To Tom

I hope you find fresh
ideas in these pages for
your journey!

From Ron Luic

9/25/12

treasure inside

23 **UNEXPECTED** Principles

That Activate **GREATNESS**

ron price

Aloha Publishing

Treasure Inside: 23 Unexpected Principles That Activate Greatness
by Ron Price

ISBN 978-1-61206-021-7

For more information, contact:
Ron Price (Author)
Price-Associates.com
TreasureInsideBook.com

Published by
ALOHA
PUBLISHING

AlohaPublishing.com

First Printing

Printed in the United States of America

*To all those with the courage and tenacity
to pursue their fullest potential.*

contents

"Everyone has inside of him a piece
of good news. The good news is that
you don't know how great you can be!
How much you can love! What you can
accomplish! And what your potential is!"
— Anne Frank

"I can't believe God put us
on this earth to be ordinary."
— Lou Holtz

"We all have possibilities
we don't know about.
We can do things we don't
even dream we can do."
— Dale Carnegie

"Ineffective people live day after day
with unused potential."
— Stephen Covey

Introduction

Dear reader,

The year is 2034. Today is an exciting day for your family. In a few hours, you will be gathered to learn the results of DNA tests for your two-year-old granddaughter. Long ago, the genome project moved out of the labs. You aren't going to the doctor's office to hear the results. Instead, this meeting will take place at the Human Individuality Institute, a private educational organization dedicated to identifying each human being's greatest future potential. By mapping and analyzing 23 pairs of chromosomes found in your granddaughter's DNA, these "personal development engineers" will predict her genetically determined interests, style, and cognitive tendencies. In other words, they will help you understand her future potential with a depth and predictability as reliable as a blood test.

Why is this important? This information about your granddaughter's genetic makeup will provide important insights that impact the types of nurturing, education, and development that will lead to realizing her greatest potential in life. It will tell you whether she should study mathematics or sociology, music or literature, whether she will thrive more in a for-profit, not-for-profit, or government career, and a whole host of other early learning choices that will greatly impact her success and contributions as an adult.

Does this sound like far-fetched science fiction? It is not. Scientists have discovered more about genetics in the last two decades than in all of the history of mankind. And their discoveries are accelerating, extending far beyond medical findings. Undoubtedly, these discoveries will one day lead to individualized development plans for the generations yet to be born.

But is potential only understood in the context of genetics? What about the importance of nurturing? Have genetics finally won the "nature versus nurture" debate? From what we have learned in the past two decades, it appears that both sides are correct. Nature (DNA) is a very potent and undeniable force, yet nurture (environment) plays an equally powerful role in the development of neural pathways, motivations, and interests during the formative years of life. Rather than view this as a competition for influence, it may be wiser for us to see these two forces as complementary. If this is the case, the greatest potential is realized when we align our education and development plans with what we have discovered through genetics.

I have spent the last 25 years exploring the "nature" part of potential, not as a scientist, but as a parent, an executive, and a business advisor. By studying potential from the early days of aptitude testing at General Electric in the 1930s to the modern application of psychometric instruments, I have pursued a comprehensive understanding of what Jim Collins refers to as "getting the right people on the bus, in the right seats." The conclusion I have come to is that talent (nature), in and of itself, is not enough. On the one hand, everyone has been endowed with a unique set of traits and tendencies that we can describe as "natural talent." On the other hand, without the disciplined nurturing of this natural talent, no one realizes anything close to his or her full potential. How much of your potential have you realized?

This is a tough question to answer. How do we know what our full potential is? We may never be able to define the full scope of human potential. But we do know what triggers, or activates, our development toward this ideal. This is the reason for *Treasure Inside: 23 Surprising Principles That Activate Greatness.* Through the pages that follow, you will discover and reflect on principles that are proven catalysts for personal growth and success.

As you read about these principles, you will learn something about my own personal journey of discovery. Included are activating principles that reflect disciplines of the mind, heart, body, and spirit. For those of you who are interested in exploring any of these principles further, or in being part of a community of like-minded individuals, there are additional resources available online at www.TreasureInsideBook.com.

The value of this book is in its capacity to activate your own introspection. What is written is significant only to the extent that it causes you to recognize the great treasure residing inside yourself and, in doing so, activate that treasure to pursue the noblest of all causes: your own highest potential.

May you enjoy your own quest for the *Treasure Inside.*

All the best,

Ron Price

P.S. For some, the inclusion of principles about spirit and faith may seem inappropriate. However, I cannot be true to my own discoveries without including them. Therefore, I reference several quotations from the Christian Bible throughout, as this is both my heritage and a great source of personal insight. However, this is not meant to be a criticism of your own personal beliefs. I have learned immeasurably from people of varying religious, as well as non-religious, persuasions.

Principle 1:
Diamonds

Russell Conwell is one of my heroes. He served in the American Civil War, worked as a lawyer and journalist, and finally settled into a career as the pastor of Baptist Temple and founder of Temple College (now Temple University). He gave the speech, "Acres of Diamonds," more than 6,000 times, probably making it the most repeated live speech in American history. The speech, which lasted longer than ninety minutes, is full of vivid examples about how often we are blind to the wealth of opportunities around us.

Below is a shortened version of the opening story of his speech:

Ladies and gentlemen:

When going down the Tigris River, we hired a guide from Baghdad to show us down to the Arabian Gulf. That guide whom we employed resembled the barbers we find in America. That is, he resembled the barbers in certain mental characteristics. He thought it was not only his duty to guide us down the river, but also to entertain us with stories. Here is one of these, which would change my perspective for the rest of my life.

He told me that there once lived an ancient Persian by the name of Al Hafed. He said that Al Hafed owned a large farm, with orchards, grain fields, and gardens. He had money at interest, had a beautiful wife and lovely children, and was a wealthy, content man.

One day, an ancient priest, one of the wise men of the East, sat down by Al Hafed's fireside and told the old farmer a life-changing tale about how diamonds were made. The old priest said, "A diamond is a congealed drop of sunlight," a statement which is literally true.

Then, the old priest said another very curious thing. He said that a diamond was the last and the highest of God's mineral creations, as a woman is the last and highest of God's animal creations. That is the reason, I suppose, why the two have such a liking for each other.

The old priest told Al Hafed that if he had a diamond the size of his thumb, he could purchase a dozen farms like his. "And," said the priest, "if you had a handful of diamonds, you could purchase the county, and, if you had a mine of diamonds, you could purchase kingdoms and place your children upon thrones, through the influence of your great wealth."

Al Hafed heard all about diamonds that night and went to bed a poor man. He wanted a whole mine of diamonds. Early in the morning, he sought the priest and awoke him. Well, I know by experience, that a priest is very cross when awakened early in the morning.

Al Hafed said, "Will you tell me where I can find diamonds?"

The priest said, "Diamonds? What do you want of diamonds?"

Said Al Hafed, "I want to be immensely rich."

"Well," said the priest, "if you want diamonds, all you have to do is to go and find them, and then you will have them."

"But," said Al Hafed, "I don't know where to go."

"If you find a river that runs over white sands and between high mountains, in those white sands you will always find diamonds," answered the priest.

"But," asked Al Hafed, "do you believe there is such a river?"

"Plenty of them; all you have to do is just go where they are."

"Well," said Al Hafed, "I will go."

So, he sold his farm, collected his money that was at interest, left his family in charge of a neighbor, and away he went in search of diamonds.

He began his search at the Mountains of the Moon. Afterwards, he came into Palestine, and then wandered on into Europe. At last, when his money was all gone and he was in rags, poverty, and wretchedness, he stood on the shore at Barcelona, in Spain, when a great tidal wave swept through the pillars of Hercules; the poor, starving, afflicted stranger could not resist the awful temptation to cast himself into that incoming tide, and he sank beneath its foaming crest, never to rise to life again.

After the old guide told that story, he stopped the camel I was riding and went back to arrange the baggage on another camel, and I had an opportunity to muse over his story.

Then, he went on:
The man who purchased Al Hafed's farm led his camel out into the garden to drink, and as the animal put his nose into the shallow waters of the garden brook, Al Hafed's successor noticed a curious flash of light from the white sands of the stream. Reaching in, he pulled out a black stone containing a strange eye of light. He took it into the house as a curious pebble and, putting it on the mantel that covered the central fire, went his way and forgot all about it.

But, not long after that, that same old priest came to visit Al Hafed's successor. The moment he opened the door, he noticed the flash of light. He rushed to the mantel and said, "Here is a diamond! Here is a diamond! Has Al Hafed returned?"

"Oh, no, Al Hafed has not returned, and we have not heard from him since he went away, and that is not a diamond. It is nothing but a stone we found out in our garden."

"'But,' said the priest, "I know a diamond when I see it. I tell you that is a diamond."

Then, together, they rushed out into the garden. They stirred up the white sands with their fingers, and there came up other, more beautiful, more valuable gems than the first.

"Thus," said the guide—and, friends, it is historically true—"was discovered the diamond mines of Golconda, the most valuable diamond mines in the history of the ancient world."

He said to me, "Had Al Hafed remained at home, and dug in his own cellar or underneath his own wheat field, instead of wretchedness, starvation, poverty, and death in a strange land, he would have had ACRES OF DIAMONDS."

Acres of diamonds! For every acre of that old farm, yes, every shovelful afterwards revealed the gems, which have since decorated the crowns of monarchs.

Principle 2:

Pressure

I love my wife. Shortly after I asked her to marry me, I suggested that we go to a jeweler to pick out a diamond engagement ring. (That should have been a clue right there that something was wrong with me—I asked her to marry me without a diamond in my pocket.)

"You don't have to do that," she said. "I don't want a diamond." I couldn't believe what I heard.

"You don't want a diamond? I've never heard of a girl not wanting a diamond!"

"Well, it's not that I don't want one—it's just that I know that you can't afford one big enough that I would want to wear," she responded.

Wow! I thought. *A realist and a pragmatist!* I could tell from the start that I would never have trouble finding out what she was thinking.

We did go to the jeweler—to buy a "moonstone," one of those big, translucent, oval-shaped, white stones. Let's just say it was an affordable option based on my available resources at the time. And my gold wedding band, which Pam purchased, cost more than her engagement ring.

For the next ten years, her comment about my inability to satisfy her taste in a diamond worked inside of me. As we started our tenth year of marriage, I put together a plan to earn extra money by doing some moonlighting, and I quietly set it aside until I had enough to go shopping. I found a modest, one-half carat diamond (enough so you could see it, but not enough to impress the real diamond chasers) in a special, antique setting, and I prepared to surprise Pam on our tenth anniversary. We traveled to The Grand Hotel on Mackinac Island, the location of Christopher Reeve's movie *Somewhere in Time*, and spent three days on the island riding horses, sampling the famous Mackinac Island fudge, and rocking on what the resort claims as the longest front porch in the world. After dinner on our final night together, I pulled out a small box wrapped in gold foil and asked Pam if she would open it. It was the best surprise I ever gave her, and, almost twenty five years later, I can still feel her response as she put this "respectable" ring on for the first time.

What makes diamonds so precious, so valued, and so extraordinary? They are unique gems, endowed with very special characteristics and uses. Industrial diamonds play a very important role in manufacturing because of their hardness and ability to cut every other material on earth, including steel. Industrial diamonds also dissipate heat very quickly. But, ultimately, the gem diamonds used in jewelry have no innate value—their value is determined entirely by those who take pleasure in purchasing and wearing them. The value of the diamond is within, but not in a "real" sense; it is valuable because people find value in it.

When I went shopping for Pam's diamond, I learned that a gem diamond is graded on its carat, clarity, color, and cut. The weight is measured by the carat, with one carat weighing two hundred milligrams. The clarity, or purity, of a gem is measured by the presence or absence of various kinds of flaws. These may include small foreign materials in the stone and small bubbles or cracks that gemologists refer to as feathers. Most diamonds have a faintly yellowish tint; a small percentage of diamonds are colorless, while a few possess a faint tinge of blue, red, brown, green, and even black.

Cutting diamonds is a painstaking, messy, and noisy business. Highly trained workers, who take many years to learn to do their work skillfully, labor in unpleasant conditions, with little room for mistakes. The cut of a gem diamond affects its value significantly, because a stone that is not properly cut at exactly the right angles does not show as much brilliance as one that is perfectly cut. The beauty of a diamond is contained, in large part, by the way it reflects light, bends rays of light, and breaks light up into all the colors of the rainbow. To produce the greatest possible brilliance, many little sides (facets) must be cut and polished at exactly the right angle.

A diamond's hardness, or toughness, is what makes it so valuable. This toughness is derived from the diamond's creation under extreme heat and pressure. The first diamonds were found in the sand and gravel of streambeds. Later, it was discovered that most diamonds are deep in the earth, in rock formations called pipes. These pipes are thought to be the throats of extinct volcanoes, and there are only four important diamond fields that have been found around the world—in Africa, India, Russia, and South America. Africa produces approximately 70 percent of the world's supply of diamonds, and Russia produces another 20 percent from the diamond fields of Siberia. Even in the most impressive fields of the world, many tons of "blue" ground must be taken from deep in the earth just to obtain one small diamond.

So, what relevance does all this information about diamonds have to our topic? Are there some parallels that we can draw from to help us as we move forward with finding the treasure inside of us?

Several years ago, one of my sons spent several weeks in Tibet, where the word for diamond means "hidden potential." In my wife's and my case, the diamond anniversary gift was representative of the hidden potential she saw in me, a man who couldn't even afford a proper ring. You see, she didn't need a diamond, because the treasure—our love—was already there. The moonstone was just a placeholder until the real thing could grace her finger. It may have taken me ten years, but it finally did.

Remember, a diamond is just a pretty stone. Its value is not inherent; it is given value by people who see value in it. Take a little time before you read on, and contemplate your own treasure inside from a new perspective.

Principle 3:
Optimism

"A group of children first visited a planetarium,
then looked at a tiny flower. Afterward they drew
on paper some of the things they had seen.
One boy put a dot in the corner of the drawing.
'This is me,' he wrote, then added thoughtfully,
'but I am bigger than the stars because I can think.'"

— Anonymous

Thoughts…have you ever wondered what role they play in our lives? Or, for that matter, where they come from? When we begin to think about thinking—a process called metacognition—we allow ourselves the opportunity to take an active role in the shaping of our lives.

Many great writers have analyzed this subject. The Bible says, "As a man thinks in his heart, so is he." (Proverbs 23:7). James Allen, a British philosopher in the 1800s, wrote a classic about this called, *As a Man Thinketh*. Ralph Waldo Emerson wrote, "A man becomes what he thinks about all day long."

He also wrote, "Great men are they who see that spiritual is stronger than any material force, **that thoughts rule the world.**"

Earl Nightingale, one of the American pioneers of personal development programs, recorded an album, *The Strangest Secret,* many years ago that resulted in the first and only gold record of a spoken presentation. He called this secret strange because it really doesn't have to be a secret at all—it is plain for everyone to see. The secret? A person becomes what he thinks about; therefore, we can change who we are and what we accomplish in life by changing what we think about.

So, how important are your thoughts and where do they come from? Another way of asking this question is, "What are your thoughts worth?" It is obvious that some people's thoughts end up being worth a fortune! And, unfortunately, we also can see that some thoughts are worth little or nothing, resulting in pain and suffering in the lives of others because of what they cause a person to become.

So, where do *your* thoughts come from?

+ Do they come from a deliberate strategy to develop your fullest potential by interacting with people who embody what you hope to become?

+ Do they come from meaningful readings, inspirational audio, or thought-provoking videos?

+ Do they come from saturating your mind with the possibilities of what could happen with your life if you gave it your best effort?

+ Do you exercise your mind by memorizing significant quotes, your mission statement, and statements of faith?

Or:

+ Do your thoughts come from indiscriminate exposure to whatever ideas, images, and fantasies Hollywood, tabloid magazines, and office gossip bring your way?

+ Do you allow your mind to be filled with scenes of violence, immoral behavior, abuse, and scandal?

+ Do you expose your precious mind to the critical- ness, negativity, resentment, despair, and fear of those around you?

The right kinds of thoughts don't come automatically in your life. You have to work at them.

Legendary golfer Arnold Palmer realizes this; he knows that his thoughts are his own and that he can shape his reality by thinking good thoughts. To help him remember this, Palmer has a single plaque hanging on a wall in his office. The plaque reveals why he has been successful on and off the golf course. It reads:

If you *think* you are beaten, you are.
If you *think* you dare not, you don't.
If you like to win but *think* you can't,
It's almost certain that you won't.

Life's battles don't always go
To the stronger woman or man,
But sooner or later, those who win
Are those who *think* they can.

Instead of being passive receptors, let's instead take an active part in shaping our thoughts—just like Arnold Palmer. Our mental processes do, after all, have the power to shape us, to create good or bad in our persons. By purposefully filling our minds with goodness, we take ownership of the nurture aspect of potential, allowing ourselves to realize our highest capabilities. Your thoughts are, quite possibly, one of the greatest powers you have today.

"Finally, brothers, whatever is true, whatever is noble, whatever is right, whatever is pure, whatever is lovely, whatever is admirable—if anything is excellent or praiseworthy—think about such things." — Paul, the Apostle, writing to the church at Philippi (Philippians 4:8)

Principle 4:
Possibilites

* Could you fulfill a secret dream if you had
  more money?

* Would you take on a new project that could
  significantly change your life if you had more time?

* What more would you attempt to do if you could
  tap into more energy?

E ach of us has a limited amount of these resources
(money, time, and energy) that provide the opportunities
for improving our lives. But, we all have some.

Some of us have extra time. Look at the time spent on
TV or the Internet, even watching spectator sports. Often
times, "not having time" for something is really not wanting
to take time away from more enjoyable activities.

Some of us have extra energy. This is why leisure and
entertainment industries continue to grow. It's also why out-
door recreation is abundantly popular in certain areas.

And, believe it or not, some people have so much money that they don't know what to do with it all. In cases such as this, consumerism is often a misguided means to personal fulfillment.

Though the vast majority of those of us living in developed nations have an abundance of these resources, it appears that we lack the wisdom to recognize how to use them to uncover and pursue our greatest potential. Moreover, these resources are often wasted; those who need them rarely get the opportunity to use or access them.

I am awestruck by the opportunities that are available to us compared with the generations that preceded us. Never before have there been as many new conveniences—the Internet, microwave ovens, etc.—to improve the quality and productivity of our lives.

Several years ago, I heard a speaker point out that the modern conveniences we enjoy in our homes represent the equivalent of approximately two hundred personal servants in ancient times. He made this proclamation before the advent of home computers, the Internet, e-mail, cell phones, online banking, and many other technologies that have connected us to an ever-expanding world of convenience and efficiency.

Never before have there been as many diversions for our time, and never before have there been as many ways to increase—and spend—our energy. Never before have there been as many charitable organizations doing as much humanitarian work. Most importantly, never before has our understanding of human potential and the path to achievement been as comprehensive as it is today.

One of the greatest demonstrations of pursuing personal potential is the story of Helen Keller. In 1882, she lost her sight and hearing, through illness, when she was only nineteen months old. Afterwards, she became a wild, rebellious, uncontrolled youngster and remained that way until a nearly blind teacher was attracted to the challenge of teaching her. As a result of Anne Sullivan Macy's belief in Helen's potential, she later attended Radcliffe College, studying French and Greek and typing her papers using a Braille typewriter. She went on to become a world-famous prodigy, raising funds for the American Foundation for the Blind, lobbying for change around the world, and brightening the spirits of wounded soldiers during World War II.

Although she lived in a world of silence and darkness, Helen Keller refused to let a disability stand in the way of her potential. She altered people's views of individuals with disabilities, while expanding the awareness of their own potential. Her greatest capacities were tapped because she never made peace with the status quo, and she never tried to be like anyone else. Instead, she invested all of her efforts toward becoming the best that she could be; she did so by thinking good thoughts and doing good deeds. Helen Keller saw herself as a change agent, having discovered the possibilities for positive change through her inner journey of self-awareness and achievement. Mark Twain said of her, "She will be as famous a thousand years from now as she is today."

What about you? What is your untapped potential? How can you convert your view of life from "what is" to "what can be"?

Winners do not leave the development of their potential to chance. They pursue it systematically with the excitement of knowing there are unlimited possibilities residing within, waiting to be discovered and put to work.

> **"The undeveloped piece of property with the greatest potential is still between the ears."**
> — Anonymous

Principle 5:
Refinement

Have you been privileged to meet and learn from great people throughout your lifetime?

In my life, some of these key individuals have been family members; they have influenced me at times when decisions were critical to my future. Some of them have been close friends who had just the right word of encouragement at the right time. Others had a word of caution when I needed a course correction.

However, many of the people who have made the greatest difference in my life have never met me face to face. They don't have the slightest idea of just how much they have changed my life. This is because many of the people who have impacted me the most are the ones I met within the books I have read.

Books are indispensable for discovering your treasure inside. In fact, I think that they are more important than any other communication medium we use. Here is why I can make that statement: in an audio or video presentation, you hear and/or see the speakers or performers, and they add their inflections, expressions, and personalities to the presentation. When you read a book, however, you become a partner with the author. The author provides the words and the rest is up to you. You read a book in your own voice, with your own inflections and nuances of awareness. It is the closest thing to experiencing the event yourself.

> The main thing that inspires me to keep reading is a desire to grow and change. Whether it is reading a book on personal development, health, or organizational management, a captivating novel, or the Bible, I'm motivated by the way books change my outlook on life. The impact of reading is immeasurable and continual; it is difficult to explain just how much it's molded my life.

You will never fully realize the great favor you are doing yourself by reading good books, regularly, over many years. Books provide food for your mind. They feed understanding, increase mental strength, inspire commitment, and refresh perspective. It is within books that we are able to fully examine ourselves without judgment, reflect without interruption, and create without pre-imposed structure. It is in the pages of a book that we often find ourselves and, in many cases, find the treasure inside.

"You are the same today as you'll be in five years except for the people you meet and the books you read."
— Charles "Tremendous" Jones, author of *Life Is Tremendous*

Principle 6:

Choices

Driving from Chicago to Detroit one afternoon, a bolt of inspiration from heaven hit me. In that moment, I discovered one of the greatest, most powerful secrets of the human journey. For the first time, I saw it clearly and recognized it so intimately that I could reach out and touch it. As I drove along, I couldn't help but picture myself opening a treasure chest. In my vision, the secret lay inside, amongst a brilliant collection of jewels and precious stones, shining bright, the rarest gem of all.

It is a hidden treasure so powerful that, once you discover it, you will have in your possession a map so clear, so defining, and so powerful that you will never go another day without finding profound opportunity. It is a treasure that is available to every living person, regardless of his or her education, past failures or successes, oppressions, or limitations. It is also one of the strangest secrets of mankind—strange because it is so obvious to those who have discovered it but secret because it remains invisible to those who have yet to understand its power.

I can't give this treasure to you, but I can show you where it is and help you understand how to uncover it so that things will never be the same. And the first step to understanding its power is to want it.

Second, you must be willing to receive it with humility. You see, without the childlike attitude of teachableness, you may scorn or ridicule this treasure and never discover the true brilliance and luster of it. Many people have found this treasure throughout history, but it was only when they set aside their cynicism and disbelief that they were able to fully utilize the miracle and mystery of this hidden treasure.

Third, you must protect it once you have found it. Its final value is not inherent; it is determined by how much value you place in it. To some, it is a small, barely noteworthy trinket of costume jewelry. For others, it revolutionizes their lives and causes them to rise to levels of success and achievement beyond their wildest dreams. This gem is so precious, yet so seldom uncovered and polished to reflect its true value.

The greatest human treasure of all is the power to choose.

That sunny afternoon, it was crystal clear: I have been given the power to choose. I don't have the power to change everything around me, but I have the power to choose how I *respond* to everything around me. I don't have the power to change people, but I have the power to change how I *respond* to people. I don't have the power to change the laws of nature, but I have the power to choose how I *employ* the laws of nature.

I have the power to choose good over evil, no matter how much evil is around me. I have the power to choose love and compassion, no matter how much criticism and resentment is around me. I have the power to choose perseverance, even if everyone else around me quits. I have the power to choose health, even if others choose disease. I have the power to choose gratitude, even if everyone else is complaining.

Yes, you, too, have the power to choose. You can choose optimism instead of pessimism. And you can choose love, joy, peace, patience, kindness, goodness, faithfulness, gentleness, and self-control (Galatians 5:22–23).

Do you get the idea? **Your future does not depend on those around you, the economy, chance, or fate. You have been given the power to choose.**

Bob Wieland had both legs blown off from a grenade that landed on him in the Vietnam War. Instead of wallowing in self-pity and defeat, Bob exercised his power to choose—and that power resulted in him setting a world record in the bench press, becoming the strength training coach for the Green Bay Packers, and running the Marine Corps Marathon in Washington, D.C., *on his hands*, all because he discovered the power to choose.

You see, we have the power to choose our actions, but none of us have the power to choose the consequences of those actions. We can choose how we respond to them, but we can't choose whether the result will be positive or negative. Bob Wieland couldn't have known that his choice to go to Vietnam would have resulted in losing his legs. We must continually utilize this treasure—the power to choose—to positively impact our situation, just as he did.

Over the years, a number of people have let me down: they abandoned me, criticized me, ignored me, and some even attacked me, but I still had the power to choose. It's the one thing that cannot be taken from me.

There have also been economic hardships throughout the years. At one point, several years ago, I lost 80 percent of my income overnight, and my wife Pam and I had to sell our house quickly to avoid bankruptcy. But, even then, we had the power to choose how we would respond and what we would do next. More recently, a career change, some poor investments, and a new business start-up drained almost all of the resources we had spent the last twenty-five years building. Once again, we were given the opportunity to choose our response to times of challenge and change.

Who knows what the future will bring? Who knows what new challenges we will face, what new trials we will endure, what suffering and hardships we must still overcome? Regardless of what will come our way, one of the greatest endowments we have during our journey on Earth is the power to choose.

How are you using this power in your life today? Have you discovered this hidden treasure within? It is your greatest resource. It holds all of the promise for your future, regardless of your age or previous experiences. It cries out within you, calling for your faith, calling for your hope, calling you to action. The greatest treasure is already within you. Open up the chest and look upon your hidden gem—you, my friend, have the power to choose.

"We can choose our thoughts, attitudes, and actions, but we cannot choose the consequences of our thoughts, attitudes, and actions, because whatever we sow will be multiplied back to us."

— Price Family

The Road Not Taken
by Robert Frost

Two roads diverged in a yellow wood,
And sorry I could not travel both
And be one traveler, long I stood
And looked down one as far as I could
To where it bent in the undergrowth;

Then took the other, as just as fair,
And having perhaps the better claim,
Because it was grassy and wanted wear;
Though as for that the passing there
Had worn them really about the same,

And both that morning equally lay
In leaves no step had trodden black.
Oh, I kept the first for another day!
Yet knowing how way leads on to way,
I doubted if I should ever come back.

I shall be telling this with a sigh
Somewhere ages and ages hence:
Two roads diverged in a wood, and I—
I took the one less traveled by,
And that has made all the difference.

Principle 7:
Visualization

"Vision...the art of seeing things invisible." That is how Jonathan Swift described it back in 1726. Peter Koestenbaum, another philosopher, wrote, "Vision is not necessarily having a plan, but having a mind that always plans. In sum, vision means to be in touch with the unlimited potential and expanse of this marvelous instrument called the human mind." Helen Keller said, "The most pathetic person in the world is someone who has sight but has no vision!"

Vision seems to be an elusive, yet important, life principle. Your vision describes the ideal future that you'd like to attain. It provides meaning and direction while rousing you to break through present limitations. Vision uses the same mental capacities as memory, which is a vivid mental picture of the past. In a sense, vision is "remembering forward" by creating a vivid mental picture of the future.

Holding a vivid picture in your mind of your desired future will unleash your creative efforts and cultivate the desire and energy necessary to perform.

Most people shy away from trying to develop a clear, dynamic vision of the future. There are many reasons for this reticence. For some, it is too scary to think about taking an active role in shaping their future. They would rather just let things happen. Many people lack the confidence that anything can change from the way it has always been. They have limited themselves by past failures and disappointments.

Others are content to move along with the rest of the crowd, never breaking away to express their unique talents or pursue their dreams. Lastly, some people think they might be offending God or somehow violating a relationship of submission and obedience by developing a vision.

Yet, a study of every great leader or achiever in history reveals the importance of vision. Effective vision is empowered by strong desire and inner drive that won't rest until it is fulfilled. This kind of vision is one of the fundamental traits shared by anyone who has ever accomplished great things. When Martin Luther King Jr. stood on the steps of the Lincoln Memorial on August 28, 1963, he proclaimed four words that have been heard around the world. "I have a dream…" was his description of a vision. The power of vision caused him to rise above racism and many other obstacles to become a leader and source of inspiration for millions around the world. The words of his speech on that day in 1963 continue to ring out again and again, encouraging us to look to the future with hope and expectation. Martin Luther King Jr.'s willingness to go after his vision gives us hope that new achievements and opportunities are waiting for us to find a similar level of commitment and bring them into reality. There are several disciplines you can employ to expand your vision.

First, read. There is so much wisdom, inspiration, and vision available in books. Biographies are particularly beneficial because they show how ordinary people often produce extraordinary results. And a well-nourished mind spawns vision.

Second, listen to recorded stories of other people's lives. We have more access to inspiring stories than at any other time in history. These audio and video programs can expose you to the ideas and experiences of ordinary people made great through extraordinary vision. Listening to inspiring life stories can tap a deep spring of creativity as you shape your vision of the future.

Third, expand your vision by keeping a journal. Writing out your thoughts, desires, needs, and dreams is invigorating. If you make journaling a regular discipline, you will engage in times of intense inspiration, thereby expanding your vision beyond anything you have ever dreamed possible. Journaling helps you focus your thoughts and crystallize the ideas that can become the core of a captivating vision.

Fourth, take time to set aside urgent, daily distractions and visualize a greater future. This will allow you quiet, reflective time to consider what possibilities your future might hold. Wrestle through what is most important in your life, what kind of person you want to become, and what great things you would attempt if you knew you could not fail. Let yourself dream; allow yourself to create a vision, a goal, for your life.

Ask yourself the following questions:

+ How would I develop a vision if I knew I could not fail?

+ If I assume my future is mine to create, how would I go about shaping my vision of the future?

+ Am I failing to define my dreams for the future because of fear or a feeling of inadequacy?

+ Do I trust myself to fate and end up surrendering to the circumstances that surround me?

+ Do I take the first step of identifying vision, only to be derailed by the onslaught of urgent activities in life?

+ Do I lose focus of what I want to become and accomplish over a long period of time?

+ What kinds of activities do I need to fill my life with to accomplish my vision?

I must admit that I have lost this focus many times. However, even with my inconsistencies, the limited clarity of vision I have experienced has given excitement and purpose to my life. Goals and desires that I thought would take a lifetime to accomplish have unfolded in a small portion of the time I expected. As I have accepted the power and opportunity inherent in "vividly imagining," I have watched change take place in my circumstances and myself far faster and to a greater degree than I thought possible. And the same can happen for you.

If you take this challenge seriously and allow yourself to create and pursue a great vision, you will enter into the greatest years of your life, with rewards beyond your imagination. Regardless of your age, wealth, education, or social standing, you can begin to create a new, exciting chapter in your life by "remembering forward."

> "If you don't know where you are going,
> you may end up somewhere else."
> — Yogi Berra

Principle 8:
Intention

Belief is key in beginning the hunt for diamonds. Unless you believe there are gems present, the work of uncovering them is too hard, too long, and too speculative. With a geologist's recommendation, you might go into your backyard and start digging for diamonds, and you may believe her for a day, a week, or maybe even a month. But, unless you understand something about the science of geology and recognize the conditions under which diamonds exist, you will begin to question her advice and quit your quest prematurely.

Until you are undone by the revelation of the infinite potential that resides within you, you cannot possibly put in the hard work necessary to do something beyond what you previously thought possible. Either you will be content maintaining your present circumstances, or, at best, you will be satisfied with just a little more. Like the analogy above, you must fully comprehend your latent potential to be able to take the steps to change your life.

Remember Al Hafed in our opening story, "Acres of Diamonds"? The storyteller told us that he "was a wealthy, content man"—until the priest told him all about diamonds. Once he learned what diamonds were and how they could change his life, we read that Al Hafed "went to bed a poor man. He wanted a whole mine of diamonds."

Hopefully, you are experiencing two essential emotions as we move forward in this book. First, my hope is that you are capturing a glimpse of your infinite potential and the great opportunity you have to blossom into someone beyond your comprehension. It is possible that you have been sparked with an excitement that has interrupted the normal routines of your day and caused you, even if only for brief moments, to experience the first, young shoots of belief in some great, overwhelming dream for your future. Second, you may feel fear and apprehension if you are really ready to pursue your emerging vision. The combination of these two emotions is one of the clearest indicators that you are tapping into your treasure inside and it's within your grasp.

Goals provide the "cutting and polishing" of your treasure inside. They take the raw material and put it to use in a productive manner, improving and enlarging your life in relation to the world around you. To use another analogy, goals harness the innate power within, much in the same way that a hydroelectric plant can turn running water into enough electrical force to light up a city. Yet, for some reason, goals are rarely utilized in most people's lives.

In light of the significant benefits of creating, writing, and pursuing goals, why don't we do these things? I am aware of at least three reasons.

First, most of us have given up on goals because we tried to write some in the past, only to be disappointed when they did not painlessly come into reality. As a result, we have become cynical about the practice of goal setting.

Second, most of us have never been taught how to write smart goals. We can write down what we want to have happen, but we don't know how to create a step-by-step blueprint that yields the end result we want.

Third, many of us have never recognized that a goal is not the true source of power for change. It is simply the mechanism through which inner power flows to facilitate change. If we haven't developed a compelling vision and recognized the power of personal choice, our goals may be empty turbines that are doomed to quit turning for lack of water flowing down the stream.

Powerful goals are not the vision; they are vehicles to pursue the vision. They contain and define our vision with a laser focus to bring about significant change in our lives.

Many speakers on effective goal setting talk about SMART goals, meaning they are:

Specific – written down in specific language so there is no question about what we seek to accomplish.

Measurable – clear quantification of what will be accomplished so there is no question when we have crossed the finish line.

Achievable – within our power and ability to accomplish.

Relevant – aligned with our values and long-term vision.

Time-bound – deadline oriented, so that various milestones and a final completion date are created.

Once you have written SMART goals, try the following ways to anchor them in your field of vision:

1. List as many benefits as you can think of for achieving each goal. Referring to this list when you are "climbing the hill" can strengthen your resolve to finish the climb in the midst of weariness, discouragement, and doubt.

2. Identify all of the obstacles you may run into during the pursuit of your goals, and create a strategy for turning these stumbling blocks into stepping-stones. One way I develop an appreciation for obstacles is by viewing them as soldiers put in the path to keep others from getting to my treasures before me.

3. Identify the new skills and knowledge you will need to develop in order to achieve your goals. A visionary goal will always require that you change and grow as an individual.

4. List the people or groups from whom you will need assistance to achieve your goals.

5. Create an accountability list of behaviors you will need to practice on a daily and weekly basis to achieve your goals. These are specific tasks that need to be completed—and often repeated—in order to move in the direction of your goal completion.

6. Create a visual representation of your goals, either in pictures or words, to keep in front of you every day so that you don't lose sight of your focus. I attach a printed copy of my goals to my car visor and read them aloud every time I get out of the car. This pushes it deep into my subconscious and keeps me centered on my aspirations.

7. Make your goals a non-negotiable priority that comes before comfort or convenience—in other words, no pleasure or leisure activities until after you have completed the daily tasks that relate to goal completion.

Years ago, advertising legend David Ogilvy set out to establish a great advertising agency within twelve years. At the time, he was a small tobacco farmer in Pennsylvania. On his second day of business, he made a list of five clients he most wanted to get. They were Bristol-Myers, Lever Brothers, Shell Oil Company, General Foods, and Campbell Soup Company. Eventually, he had them all.

When you have created an ambitious vision and immersed yourself in the revelation of your hidden treasures, SMART goals will provide you with the focus and game plan to make the impossible come true.

"The future does not get better by hope, it gets better by plan. And to plan for the future we need goals."

— Jim Rohn, motivational speaker

Principle 9:
Providence

What does commitment mean to you? What role does commitment play in your life? How much power comes from the commitments you make?

Many psychologists believe that our inner capacity and self-esteem are directly related to our commitments. They observe that people who make and keep commitments to themselves consistently have more self-confidence than those who live in the arena of wishful thinking or leave a long trail of broken promises. They have also concluded that, if you want to increase your level of confidence and self-esteem, it begins with making and keeping commitments to yourself. Because of this, they recommend creating *short-term* goals that you have a 90 percent chance of achieving. Though these goals may not seem very demanding, each fulfilled goal adds a new thread into the fabric of your self-confidence and increases your ability to respond favorably to new opportunities.

Unfortunately, there are many obstacles to commitment in our culture today—so many options, so many distractions, and so many excuses for not staying true to your commitments.

These hindrances can challenge your resolve and often create rips in the fabric of your character. When character is weakened, destiny is also changed, usually for the worse.

There is power in commitment, and high achievers give commitment a very high priority. Henry Emerson Fosdick, an American clergyman and author, wrote, "No steam or gas ever drives anything until it is confined. No Niagara [Falls] is ever turned into light and power until it is tunneled. No life ever grows until it is focused, dedicated, and disciplined."

NFL coach, Dick Vermeil, summed up his feelings about commitment by saying, "If you don't invest very much, then defeat doesn't hurt very much and winning is not very exciting." So, if we are not fully committed to something, then we do not get to experience the full joy of success.

Think of the late Mary Kay Ash, who started a new business in 1963 with $5,000 and a vision for how she could give women unlimited opportunity. The power of her commitment led to what has become one of the largest direct sales companies in the United States. With more than two million global independent sales representatives, her $5,000 investment has grown into a business that does more than $2.5 billion in global wholesale sales each year! Her commitment led her to achieve greatness.

What power would be released into your life if you decided that, from this day forward, you would never make another commitment without a deliberate decision to absolutely fulfill it? Bill Cosby once said, "Anyone can dabble, but once you've made that commitment, then your blood has that particular thing in it, and it's very hard for people to stop you." Commitment really does make things happen.

My favorite quote on the power of commitment comes from Johann Wolfgang von Goethe, a poet and playwright who had as much significance in Germany as Shakespeare had in England:

> Until one is committed there is hesitancy, the chance to draw back, always ineffectiveness. Concerning all acts of initiation (and creation) there is one elementary truth, the ignorance of which kills countless ideas and splendid plans. That the moment one definitely commits oneself then providence moves too. All sorts of things occur to help one that would never otherwise have occurred. A whole stream of events issues from the decision raising in one's favor all manner of unforeseen incidents and meetings and material assistance which no man could have dreamt should come his way. Whatever you can do or dream, you can begin it. Boldness has genius, power and magic in it. Begin it now!

Ken Blanchard explains it this way: "There's a difference between interest and commitment. When you're interested in doing something, you do it only when it's convenient.

When you're committed to something, you accept no excuses, only results."

Vision, goals, choice, and commitment—these are the ultimate diamonds of the mind. When you discover them within and learn how to cut and polish them, they will bring you acres and acres of diamonds.

Principle 10:
Intensity

"Most of the significant things done in the world
were done by persons either too busy or too sick!
There are few ideal and leisurely settings
for the disciplines of growth."
— Robert Thornton Henderson, Presbyterian theologian

Strong desire is a potent thing. No adult can ignore the power with which a favored child or grandchild can get what he or she wants, with simply a captivating smile and tenacious spirit. Children that are particularly predisposed to using desire as a tool in their quest for fulfillment (getting what they want) are often called "strong willed." When they are young, we vacillate between considering this a character strength or a dangerous flaw to be corrected. However, most anyone who has ever achieved anything of lasting significance has demonstrated similar tenacity.

When it comes to the pursuit of dreams, intense desire is the highest rated fuel for success. Virtually all lasting change and personal development begins with intense desire. We change a habit, job, or vision for our lives when our desire for change exceeds the inertia of our current circumstances. Quitting smoking, losing weight, starting an exercise program, or launching a new business are all actions that are initiated from a desire within. Our ability to follow through is almost always dependent on the intensity of that desire.

Strong desire is also the resource we depend on to "keep going" when everyone else quits because of weariness. Often, those around us misunderstand our goals and dreams. They either question the reasonableness of our dreams or they resent our attempts to break free from the inertia they have accepted as inevitable. Because they don't see what we see, or feel our desire, they criticize and often ridicule our new steps toward freedom.

Intense desire can also be frightening. It confronts another strong emotion that tries to control a person's destiny: fear of failure. For some folks, the battle between the two emotions is too great, and they surrender to the feelings of inadequacy and low self-esteem. For those willing to embrace risk and uncertainty, however, this strong desire empowers them to find a way to succeed.

You'll often hear it said that the people who are the "best" at something are not always the most successful; ability isn't much without discipline, drive, and follow-through. The real winners in life are not those with the most talent, the highest education, or the greatest opportunities. They are those who are propelled into dynamic, exciting experiences as a result of a driving desire and unending pursuit of their dreams.

How can you begin to cultivate the kind of powerful desire that will transform your future? Try developing an emotional expression of your sense of purpose. Mission statements start with determining what you deeply care about and want to accomplish in your life. An emotionally powerful mission statement is simple, yet meaningful. Begin by writing several paragraphs about what is most important to you, and then look for a succinct, passionate way to communicate the core of your purpose through one phrase. Make it short enough to be memorizable, but long enough to accurately express your life's purpose.

Here are some examples of mission statements:

+ To continuously improve the lives of those I love.
+ To experience and reflect the glory of God in every area of my life.
+ To pursue the best and noblest in personal achievement.
+ To attain excellence and become the best in

  _____.
+ To create a life of unconditional love.

When simply read on a page, none of these phrases will automatically create deep desire. When a phrase captures the heart of your purpose, however, it becomes an emotional expression of the empowering desire within. Remember, desire and focus must go hand-in-hand. Writing down your mission statement—your life's purpose—will help you maintain the child-like tenacity needed to achieve your goals and dreams. It is this deep treasure of intense desire that actively crafts a future of greatness and a unique life journey.

"You do not succeed because you do not know what you want, but because you don't want it intensely enough."

— Frank Crane, journalist

Principle 11:

Discontentment

What events in your life have provided the greatest motivation for change?

What relationships have triggered your best growth as an individual?

When are you more focused on creativity and finding new solutions?

When do you find the inspiration to create and pursue an important goal?

If you take a moment to carefully consider these questions, you will probably find that your answers center around a common theme: discontentment.

We are creatures of comfort and convenience. We instinctively work to create a routine that is predictable and provides us with enough of what we want to make life enjoyable; we refer to this as our comfort zone. When this status quo is interrupted, for any reason, our immediate response is to work on restoring stability in our lives. Yet, in our rush for security, we often miss a greater treasure waiting to be discovered.

In moments of discontentment, there is often opportunity for great growth.

There are many needs in our lives and, consequently, several opportunities for discontentment. The first and most crucial need is physical. This includes food, rest, shelter, health, and safety. These are usually the most obvious sources of discontentment; if we aren't satisfying these needs, other needs are usually secondary. Satisfaction of these needs requires money—and, even though many people wish life wasn't so complicated by the need to earn and manage money, very little can be accomplished without it. Discontentment with finances is a tricky motivator for many people. Some get carried away over the pursuit of money, while others appear to be afraid of it. Yet, whether you approach money as a tycoon or a monk, physical needs cannot be met without it, and discontentment with physical circumstances nearly always leads to a pursuit of more money.

The second need is social, or relational. We seek companionship, assistance, encouragement, and love in our relationships. In fact, aspiring to vitality and fulfillment in this area is often our greatest challenge, particularly in relationships in which we feel stuck, such as at work or home. When a relationship results in tension, misunderstanding, exploitation, or resentment, the "fight or flight" syndrome ensues. Discontentment with stressful or dysfunctional relationships is a powerful stimulus for change. Exercising the courage necessary to deal with uncomfortable circumstances can result in reconciliation or changes that can open up new possibilities for love, care, and understanding—all positive outcomes of discontentment.

Discontentment also works to stimulate our third need, intellectual development. In each of us is an innate need to grow, explore, and learn. This need isn't as obvious or demanding as our physical and relational needs, but it is a prevailing force just the same. Unfortunately, too many people feed their mental appetites with intellectual "junk foods," such as current event magazines, trashy novels, and an endless lineup of useless Internet sites, television shows, and movies. These things lead people to become addicted to cerebral stimulations that do little to create growth. In doing so, thoughts are stunted and subdued as the brain is fed only negativity and Hollywood manufactured stimuli. When discontentment with our current life situation leads to motivation, real, positive changes can begin to occur.

Fourth, a subtle and sometimes elusive area of discontentment is unfulfilled spiritual needs. Most everyone possesses a yearning to make a difference in the life of someone else. If we don't discover and express this need to make a contribution, discontentment will result. Often, this is the most difficult need to identify because it seems paradoxical: we have a need (selfish) to contribute to the lives of others (unselfish). Yet, many people who satisfy their physical, relational, and intellectual needs continue to live in quiet desperation because of well-camouflaged spiritual discontentment. This dissatisfaction often serves in our search for God, some greater purpose for our lives, or an opportunity to make a lasting impact in the lives of others. Without this discontentment, we would end up moving through the seasons of life without the nobility of purpose that gives meaning to our existence.

Of course, any of these areas of discontentment can get out of balance, driving us to pursue one particular need beyond what is healthy or beneficial in our lives. However, without a reasonable amount of discontentment, we would never stretch beyond our comfort zone to discover new possibilities and explore the almost limitlessness of our potential. That is why I am very grateful for the blessing of discontentment.

What about you? Are there some areas of discontentment in your life? If so, don't feel guilty or resentful. Instead, recognize the tremendous blessing of your discontentment, and start developing a plan to use it as a catalyst for change.

"Crisis can have value because
it generates transformation."
— John Sculley, author and business executive

Principle 12:
Pain

If discontentment is an inner voice clamoring for change, then pain is the trumpet blast. Acute pain, above all else, demands a response from us. People will do almost anything and go anywhere to get rid of acute pain. Whether physical, emotional, intellectual, or spiritual, acute pain dominates our consciousness until we find relief.

Having moved into middle age, I'm surprised at how much I'm willing to put up with chronic physical pain. I may wake up with sore muscles from the previous day's tennis match, suffer with a dull headache from dehydration or tension, or tolerate an aching joint. Most of the time, I don't think anything of it; I just accept it as part of life. As long as it doesn't become acute, I wait for my body to resolve whatever the problem may be. It seems that, as we grow older, we condition ourselves to accept chronic pain and learn to live with it as a reasonable part of life. Even when we do respond to acute physical pain, most of us show little concern for its cause as long as we can find immediate relief. After all, we don't take aspirin for a headache because we suffer from an aspirin deficiency.

I suspect the same principle follows suit in the other compartments of our lives, whether they are emotional, intellectual, or spiritual. And if we can have emotional, intellectual, and spiritual needs, then we can also have pain in these areas, too. We may be vaguely aware of chronic pain in these areas from time to time, but, for the most part, we carry on without giving it much attention, anticipating that it will work itself out over time. When the pain becomes acute, we focus only on eliminating the immediate crisis, and we seldom probe deeper to uncover the underlying cause of our emotional, intellectual, or spiritual pain.

In many instances, especially with physical pain, this wait-and-see approach is the best course of action. However, the medical advances of the last twenty-five years have taught us of another, more valuable purpose for pain.

We have learned that pain is often the messenger of a deeper systemic problem that, if not addressed at the root cause, results in serious consequences.

When we have physical pain of increasing intensity, most of us employ graduated tactics of response. First, we rest. Then, we may attempt to self-medicate. If the pain is acute enough and persists, we visit our primary healthcare provider. Sometimes, we are passed along to one or more specialists. The goal of this progression is first to eliminate the pain and, when it appears more serious, to identify and treat the underlying cause.

How often do you follow a similar blueprint when responding to a non-physical pain or problem? It is really easy to follow the same course of non-action or let it "work itself out." I don't like problems. So, whenever I have a problem, the first thing I do is ignore it and hope it goes away. If it persists and becomes acute, I try to quickly fix it myself. If that fails, I solicit the assistance of my family or close friends. Only when a problem reaches the crisis level do I look for professional help.

In our efforts to ignore our problems, most of us generally don't think of them as friends. And we most assuredly don't refer to them as treasures. Instead, they are irritations to be ignored or eliminated as soon as possible. But, what if problems are messengers of a deeper condition? What if they exist to teach us something of greater value?

Consider what sages have written about pain. In *Success Through a Positive Mental Attitude*, Napoleon Hill wrote, "Every adversity, every failure and every heartache carries with it the seed of an equivalent or a greater benefit." Furthermore, M. Scott Peck, author of *The Road Less Traveled*, wrote, "It is in the whole process of meeting and solving problems that life has meaning. Problems are the cutting edge that distinguishes between success and failure. Problems call forth our courage and our wisdom; indeed, they create our courage and our wisdom. It is only because of problems that we grow mentally and spiritually. It is through the pain of confronting and resolving problems that we learn." To these men, pain isn't a problem. It is a necessity—something we need to grow as human beings.

This is not my normal response to problems. I intellectually accept that problems are a part of life; I also acknowledge that problems stimulate growth by teaching us new ways of doing things. If problems really do contain treasures, how are we to uncover them? How can we convert this pain into gain? I believe that the answers to these two questions lie in learning to analyze problems and tap into the energy within them. This energy, if released, will bring significant changes.

Instead of minimizing or brushing aside a problem, we need to intensify it, define it, and get to the core of it. As with physical pain, our first instinct is to fixate on the symptom of our emotional, intellectual, or spiritual pain. We just want the symptom to go away, but we don't care about, or look for, the cause. It is only after the symptoms persist that we start to probe deeper. Even then, it is only when we intensify our awareness of the problem that we release the energy pent up for its resolution. In doing so, we uncover the personal impact of the problem, identify its source, and work to heal the pain, not just treat it. This requires self-awareness and reflection that is truly focused on finding the cause of suffering and working to eradicate that cause. Then, and only then, can we be free of pain.

What pains hold treasures for you? What suffering is great enough to motivate change? What problems have become acute enough that you are ready to quit tolerating them and start taking action to overcome them? Instead of ignoring or denying pain, why not allow it to enrich your life by unleashing the power within?

"The best years of your life are the ones in which you decide your problems are your own. You don't blame them on your mother, the ecology or the president. You realize that you control your own destiny."

— Albert Ellis, clinical psychologist

Principle 13:
Enthusiasm

Henry Chester called it "the greatest asset in the world," saying that it "beats money, power and influence." Ralph Waldo Emerson said that every great and commanding movement in the history of the world was a result of it. Emory Ward likened it to "measles, mumps, and the common cold; it's highly contagious." J. Paul Getty ranked it ahead of imagination, business acumen, and ambition. What is it? The power of enthusiasm.

Edward Butler wrote, "Every man is enthusiastic at times. One man has enthusiasm for 30 minutes, another man has it for 30 days. But it is the man who has it for 30 years who makes a success of life." What is this quality of character, this wonderful asset we call "enthusiasm"?

The word comes from the Greek *entheos*, which means to have "God within." It's an inner flame of excitement that causes us to hold our heads up and walk a little quicker and lighter, while creating a sparkle in our eyes. Charles Kingsley said, "We act as though comfort and luxury were the chief requirements of life, when all that we need to make us happy is something to be enthusiastic about."

But, for enthusiasm to be real, it can't be a gimmick. It can't be a mask we put on to make other people think everything is okay on the inside. For enthusiasm to be effective, it must be authentic. We must truly aspire to accomplish something worth accomplishing and, in doing so, throw our whole energy into it.

For me, enthusiasm begins by careful contemplation. I ask myself, " Is this project or goal something I can stay excited about long enough to complete? Is it worthy of my devotion, my energy, and my resources? Is it worth everything it will take to overcome the obstacles I'm bound to run into along the way?" If the answer is yes, then it's time for me to get excited—and stay excited—no matter what obstacles come up.

Please don't misinterpret what I am saying. To tap the power of enthusiasm doesn't require a lifetime commitment, unless the goal is a lifetime goal. You can practice enthusiasm in even the most ordinary things, and the immense power of enthusiasm can work wonders for you. You can clean the basement with an attitude of drudgery, and it can be one of the longest days of your life. Or, you can choose to be enthusiastic about what the basement is going to look like when you are finished. It's not the task or goal but, rather, the approach you use to accomplish it. Garnering that inner motivation and enthusiasm can help you find joy in otherwise unpleasant work.

As a young boy, I had a relative who my family respected because of his cool, reserved demeanor. He was quiet, never showed much emotion, and tended to respond to excitement with skepticism and a slightly sarcastic sense of humor. I can remember wanting to be like him when I grew up because he seemed to be cool and "in control." Now, after fifty-eight years of living, I have concluded that it was poor judgment on my part to want to emulate his approach to life. Instead, I've decided to become a kid again, to get excited about the great things happening in my life, and to stay excited about my vision for a continuously improving future. I want to get excited about a beautiful sunrise coming over the mountains, reflecting off the lake on the back deck of our home. I want to get excited about the brilliance of the stars on a warm, summer night. I want to get excited about the privilege of growing, loving relationships with my children. And, I want to get excited about focusing my efforts on making a difference in the lives of others. As Thomas Huxley said, "The secret of genius is to carry the spirit of the child into old age, which means never losing your enthusiasm."

If enthusiasm isn't the dominant emotion rising from your heart every morning, there are ways you can change. Make a deliberate decision to turn away from the negative thoughts, attitudes, and behaviors that rob you of a continuous expectation for good in your life. Retrain your mind to focus on positive, admirable thoughts and attitudes; when you notice a negative thought, behavior, or emotion, focus on transforming it into a positive one. Act enthusiastic, for our emotions cannot hold two opposites at the same time. If you act enthusiastic, in time, you will be enthusiastic.

Henry David Thoreau took this idea to heart. He used to lay in bed in the morning, telling himself all the good news he could think of: that he had a healthy body, his mind was alert, his work was interesting, the future looked bright, and a lot of people trusted him. He then rose to meet the day in a world filled with good things, good people, and good opportunities. He activated enthusiasm before beginning his day. In doing so, Thoreau took responsibility for his own level of enthusiasm.

But, don't try to use enthusiasm to impress others. This is insincere, and it will backfire. Instead, make it your goal to build enthusiasm within yourself. This deep, heart-generated enthusiasm will come out naturally, genuinely, to make you more attractive and interesting to others. Whom would you rather be with: someone who exudes vitality, enthusiasm, and a zest for life or a pessimistic, downtrodden, boring individual? When given the choice, most people would rather befriend the optimistic, enthusiastic, upbeat person.

principle 13: enthusiasm

Enthusiasm is a continuously renewable resource: the more you draw on it, the more you will have. It will find solutions where there appear to be none. And it will achieve success when success was considered impossible.

The irresistible power of enthusiasm...make sure you get your fill of it today!

"People who are unable to motivate themselves
must be content with mediocrity, no matter
how impressive their other talents."

— Andrew Carnegie

Principle 14:
Persistence

Sir Winston Churchill took three years to pass eighth grade because he had trouble learning English. Ironically, years later, Oxford University asked him to address its commencement ceremony. He arrived with his usual props: a cigar, a cane, and a top hat, which accompanied Churchill wherever he went. As Churchill approached the podium, the crowd rose in appreciative applause. With unmatched dignity, he settled the crowd and stood confidently before his admirers. Removing the cigar from his mouth and carefully placing the top hat on the podium, Churchill gazed at his waiting audience. Authority rang in Churchill's voice as he shouted, "Never give up!" Several seconds passed before he rose to his toes and repeated, "Never give up!" His words thundered in their ears. There was a deafening silence as Churchill reached for his hat and cigar, steadied himself with his cane, and left the platform. His commencement address was finished.

There is probably no better example than Winston Churchill of the power of persistence. But, there are still many other good examples. Dr. Seuss, for instance, was rejected by

27 publishers before his first book, *And to Think That I Saw It on Mulberry Street*, was finally accepted. The twenty-eighth publisher sold six million copies, and Dr. Seuss died knowing that his perseverance resulted in entertaining, challenging, and educating millions of children.

Still, there are more examples. Henry Ford went bankrupt twice during his first three years in the automobile business, but he didn't give up. Vince Lombardi didn't become a coach in the NFL until he was forty-seven. Michelangelo endured seven years of lying on his back on a scaffold to paint the Sistine Chapel.

Charles Goodyear was obsessed with the idea of making rubber unaffected by temperature extremes. Years of unsuccessful experimentation caused bitter disappointment, imprisonment for debt, family difficulties, and ridicule from his friends. He persevered and, in February 1839, Goodyear discovered that adding sulfur to rubber achieved his goal of manufacturing safe tires.

One of my favorite examples of perseverance involves a man who didn't seem to understand limitations and continuously reached higher than his colleagues thought appropriate. He:

- **Failed in business at the age of 22,**
- **Was defeated for the State Legislature at the age of 23,**
- **Failed again in business at the age of 24,**

+ Was elected to the Legislature at the age of 25,
+ Lost his sweetheart to death at the age of 26,
+ Had a nervous breakdown at the age of 27,
+ Lost an election for speaker of the State Legislature at the age of 29,
+ Lost an election to become an elector at the age of 31,
+ Was defeated for the House of Representatives at the age of 34,
+ Was elected to the House of Representatives at the age of 37,
+ Was defeated for the House of Representatives at the age of 39,
+ Was defeated for the Senate at the age of 46,
+ Was defeated for the vice presidency at the age of 47,
+ Was defeated again for the Senate at the age of 49,
+ And was elected President of the United States at the age of 51.

That's the resume of Abraham Lincoln! Imagine what courage and perseverance it must have taken to endure so many defeats and still keep marching in the direction of his vision for his life. The list above probably isn't all of his defeats. These are just the "public" defeats he endured that everyone around him knew about.

The stories go on and on. In case after case, persistence was a vital ingredient for success and greatness.

Harriet Beecher Stowe said it this way: "When you get into a tight place and everything goes against you, until it seems that you could not hold on a minute longer, never give up then for that is just the place and time that the tide will turn." President Calvin Coolidge wrote, "Nothing in the world can take the place of persistence. Talent will not; nothing is more common than unsuccessful people with talent. Genius will not; unrewarded genius is almost a proverb. Education will not; the world is full of educated derelicts. Persistence and determination alone are omnipotent."

In spite of all of the compelling stories and quotes about perseverance, it is still one of the rarest of qualities. Granted, most of us don't give up in dramatic ways—instead, we usually find quiet, subtle ways to turn away from our dreams of greatness, to settle for a life of convenience and mediocrity. Sometimes, our compromise is so subtle that even we don't realize that we lost the zeal for greatness that once captured our imaginations. When this occurs, we stop the faithful execution of the activities, discipline, and perseverance necessary to bring our dreams into reality.

Several years ago, I became curious about the antithesis of persistence and how prevalent it seems to be in our society. I was surprised to learn that almost everyone thinks about quitting. Employees often think about quitting their jobs, business owners often think about quitting (or selling) their businesses, pastors and priests often think about quitting the ministry, politicians often think about quitting public service, and couples often think about quitting their marriages.

Often times, people seriously consider quitting because they see themselves as victims. They feel that outside forces of one type or another make it too difficult for them to continue to pursue their dreams. Employees complain about bosses and company policies that conflict with their values. Business owners complain about competition and overregulation. Religious leaders complain about complacency and the pressures of performing in ministry. Politicians complain about media and campaign demands. Couples complain about dysfunctional relationships or lost romance. In every instance, the common thread is that feeling of powerlessness against external forces that have destroyed the idealism that once guided a strong sense of purpose.

Of course, there are some instances where giving up is the appropriate thing to do. If and when we realize that the target we set for our lives is wrong, or that those we love are being hurt by our persistence, the noble thing to do may be to quit. Maybe our purpose has lost its moral integrity through a series of mistakes and poor judgment. Perhaps demands from others have emerged that challenge us to compromise our character and ethical core in order to continue. These are all legitimate reasons to quit and rethink our goals and dreams.

More often, however, we drift away from our goals and commitments because they are more difficult than we originally envisioned. It's taking us longer than we expected, we aren't getting the results as easily as we had hoped, or we discover that we don't have all of the skills we need to achieve our goals. Sometimes, we drift because of criticism from others or, worse yet, because of self-criticism that decimates our self-confidence. We become discouraged because others have let us down. Or, maybe we didn't realize that the pursuit of a certain goal was going to be an uphill journey—all the way! Even though these are the most common reasons why people cease to persevere, none of them are good reasons to quit.

So, how can you reinvigorate your resolve? I suggest three steps to strengthen your ability to persevere. If practiced daily, these three steps can help keep you from discouragement and strengthen your persistence:

Renew your vision. Keeping the big picture in mind will reiterate that whatever price you have to pay is worth it. You can do this through a life mission statement and a set of lifetime goals. [3]

Sharpen your focus. Consciously and deliberately choose activities that will move you forward in your dreams. In doing so, a sharpened focus will help you intentionally say "no" to activities, interests, and sensory stimulations that compete for your energy.

Cultivate the habit of thankfulness. Thankfulness is the greatest weapon we have in the battle against discouragement.

---

[3] See Principle 10, "Desire."

Remember, a person cannot hold two opposite attitudes or emotions at the same time. For instance, you can't be happy and angry simultaneously. In order to experience one emotion, you have to give up the other. So, if you make a daily habit of cultivating thankfulness, if you are constantly looking for new reasons to be thankful, and if you learn to be genuinely thankful in every circumstance, there will no longer be any room for discouragement.

John D. Rockefeller said, "I do not think there is any other quality so essential to success of any kind as the quality of perseverance. It overcomes almost everything, even nature." Persistence is an inner resource—it comes only from your heart and must be cultivated, encouraged, and strengthened daily to have its full effect.

Principle 15:
Listening

A re you interested in developing one skill that is guaranteed to improve every other aspect of your life? This skill can affect everything from your success in business to your closest relationships and happiness. It is a simple skill, but not necessarily easy. It is challenging, but the rewards for making it a central part of your life are immeasurable. It is the most important skill used by everyone from a concert violinist to a top salesperson. It will turn enemies into friends, skeptics into believers, and product presentations into profitable sales.

Listening and understanding others is the cornerstone on which every truly professional person builds her success. Yet, it is also one of the primary stumbling blocks for those who have not yet learned its importance.

So many benefits come to a highly advanced listener. When you are able to put this treasure into practice, it can become one of your greatest strengths, and you will see a whole new world that you didn't realize existed before. Other people will suddenly enjoy being around you; they will readily share their needs with you and reveal many ways that you can fulfill your goals. Intent listening shows others how much you care, and they are more likely to take a new interest in what you know. When others know that you have listened and understood them deeply, they will be less likely to feel like you are just trying to sell them something or control them. Even better, the greatest benefit of all is that you will be changed by listening effectively to others.

Of course, any skill can be executed correctly or incorrectly, but listening will increase the likelihood of success. What are some of the mistakes we make in listening to others? Probably the biggest is when we "listen to respond." This means that, instead of patiently considering and reflecting on what another person is saying, we immediately begin formulating a response in our minds while they are still speaking. We then take the first available opportunity to interrupt and begin vocalizing our thoughts. This approach to listening creates more frustration than anything else. The person we speak to walks away thinking that we don't care enough to listen closely; this response-focused listening causes him to conclude that his concerns have not been understood enough to help him in any significant way.

The second mistake is listening to argue. This is very similar to listening to respond, but it is a little more aggressive. We might take the time to listen to what the other person is saying, but our motive all the while is to find a vulnerable spot in her position. Our focus, in this case, is to win a debate or prove our superior mental capacities. When we approach listening in this way, we fail to see the deeper purpose in communicating. Our ability to influence or persuade is anchored to our ability to first understand a person's point of view and the reason she feels the way she does.

The third mistake we make is listening autobiographically. This means that we allow the words we hear to trigger similar memories, and we then link the speaker's words or ideas to our own experiences. This type of listening is exposed by phrases like, "I know what you mean. That is the same thing that happened to me when..." But, do we really know that it is the same thing? Our situation may be similar to the speaker's, but it can never be exactly the same. When we make this autobiographical link, we are ignoring a greater opportunity to understand what was unique about the other person's experience.

History teaches us that Winston Churchill's greatest attribute was his bulldogged stubbornness. However, those close to him admired what an effective listener he was. He never cut off a suggestion with a curt dismissal and always encouraged elaboration. In doing so, he sought to gain a deeper understanding of why the speaker felt as he did.

Here are some simple steps we can take that will help us grow bigger ears and hearts, empowering us to become more valuable to others and, in turn, increase our own happiness and success:

1. Repeat what the other person says to you. It may seem silly to do this, but it is a surefire way to break the bad habit of listening to respond. By repeating the exact words you hear as closely as possible, you increase your listening capacity. Of course, it may not always be appropriate to repeat what you have heard word-for-word. Nonetheless, this discipline will help you focus your attention more on listening—and less on how you want to respond.

2. After achieving a measure of success with this kind of listening, the next step is to repeat the content of what is being said, using different words. This forces you to take another step in the listening process, teaching you to think through the content of what the person is saying. It also helps to demonstrate your sincere desire to understand him thoroughly before responding. Once again, it will impede autobiographical listening and heighten your senses to information that may have otherwise gone unnoticed.

3. The next step in quality listening is to restate the way the other person is feeling. It isn't enough to just hear words or even change the words without losing content. It is only when we begin to hear the heart that we truly begin to understand the whole person. Can you internalize and restate the emotions the person is feeling? Are deeper needs being revealed

beyond the words? These are questions to use in order to identify more closely with what is unique in the speaker's experience.

Unless we take the time to hear others at a heart level (which is achieved by engagement at an emotional level), we understand only a small portion of what we should. Even if I might be able to anticipate what the other person wants to say, he still needs to say it. Effective listening demands patience.

Here is the final indicator of effective listening: Could you be an advocate for the other person's point of view?

It doesn't matter whether you agree or disagree with what she is saying. Do you understand it well enough that she would trust you to represent her position to another person? This is a valuable exercise in selling, negotiating, and reconciling differences.

Most of the time, people think that we disagree because we don't fully understand them. If we can show that we understand well enough to represent their position, even if we don't agree, they will often be more open to being influenced by a different opinion. Many times, listening and probing for deeper understanding will result in others discovering deeper truths without us saying anything.

> "Big people monopolize the listening.
> Small people monopolize the talking."
> — David Schwartz, author of *The Magic of Thinking Big*

Principle 16:
Friendship

Friendship is not so much about finding people who will like and support you; instead, it is a treasure that empowers you to like and support them. Dale Carnegie said, "You can make more friends in two months by becoming interested in other people than in two years by trying to get other people interested in you." In order to have friends, then, you must be a friend worth having.

Friendship is truly a prized treasure of the heart. It has been described as a "treasure ship anyone can launch." Seth Parker wrote,

> The happiest business in all the world is that of
>   making friends,
> And no investment on the street pays larger
>   dividends,
> For life is more than stocks and bonds, and love
>   than rate percent,
> And he who gives in friendship's name shall reap
>   what he has spent.

What he says is true—give of yourself, and it will come back tenfold.

I took a yearlong sabbatical several years ago while transitioning between careers. For the summer months, one of my goals (much to my wife's chagrin) was to finally learn how to play golf. I mean really play golf. I bought two highly recommended instruction books, spent a considerable amount of time at the driving range, and had a standing golf appointment with a good friend every Monday morning while everyone else was beginning a new week of work.

Occasionally, I would play a round all by myself, just because I wanted to play and everyone else was at work. One quiet, midweek afternoon, I was playing the eleventh hole of my favorite course, hitting my third shot on a very difficult par four that I don't think I had ever played in less than five strokes. My shot was approximately 85 yards from the hole, and I chose a pitching wedge and swung away, hoping to land on or near the green. My ball took a steep ascent toward the green and, much to my amazement, plummeted into the hole without ever touching the green. I was dumbfounded! I dropped my golf club in amazement and wondered, *What do I do now?* Without a doubt, it was the most remarkable moment in my mediocre attempts at golf, and there I stood—alone. Nobody saw what happened but me. Nobody was there to cheer for me. And nobody watched me walk up to the hole, bend down, and pull the ball out of the hole while the flagstick remained in place.

This is one of the more memorable, albeit frivolous, examples of the value of friendship in my life. We have all experienced more significant times when friendship was precious to us—celebrating some great milestone, mourning a painful loss, or just sitting on the deck on a warm, summer evening, reminiscing about old times. It's truly a treasure to share these moments with friends.

One of the greatest "friends" I have ever met is the late Charlie "Tremendous" Jones. He picked up the middle name "Tremendous" years ago on the speaking circuit because, no matter what question you asked him, his answer was always, "Tremendous!" Charlie could count thousands of friends on almost every continent on earth. Why? Because Charlie Jones *was* a friend everywhere he went—and it came enthusiastically from his heart. One of his favorite stories was about hugging and greeting hundreds of people after a talk one night in Minneapolis. Several weeks later, he received a letter. It read, "You will remember me—I'm the older gentleman you hugged after your speech in Minneapolis. I just wanted you to know that you are the first person who has ever hugged me in my entire life."

What kind of a friend are you?

Friendship is faithful. By listening, caring, and helping, you add strength and stability to another person's life.

Friendship is kind. By giving attention and encouragement that cannot be purchased, you validate a person's unique worth.

Friendship is loyal. By not talking behind a person's back differently than you speak of him in his presence, you esteem him.

Friendship is compassionate. By standing with a person through difficulty and loss, you help preserve him.

Friendship is forgiving. By not counting a person's transgressions against him, you help restore him.

Friendship is gentle. By reaching out to a person in trouble, you help redeem him.

Friendship is sacrificial. Jesus said, "Greater love has no one than this, that he lay down his life for his friends" (John 15:13).

Friendship is about giving—the more you give it, the more you will receive. If you want to optimize the diamond of friendship in your heart, be a friend to more than those who are just like yourself. Have some friends who are old and some who are young. Have friends you look up to for guidance and some who do the same with you. Have friends you work with and some you play with, some who listen and some who speak. Have liberal friends as well as conservative friends and some who come from different cultures and creeds as well. Finally, have friends whom you can feel safe with, having neither to weigh your thoughts nor measure your words when you are with them.

> **"The only way to have a friend is to be a friend."**
>
> — Ralph Waldo Emerson

Principle 17:

Energy

E nergy is the source that drives life forward. Our personal energy comes from a number of different sources. We all create and consume intellectual, emotional, spiritual, and physical energy. Energy is a catalyst for all of the other principles that activate greatness. However, the energy that comes from our physical practices is a modern challenge, taking on a higher importance as more of us move from physical to mental work.

Early in my career, I co-owned four truck tire retreading facilities with my father. We were small business owners, which meant we did whatever work was necessary in the business, including throwing around 100 pound truck tires and hundreds of boxes of tread rubber, as well as swinging 15-pound sledgehammers continually to break tires loose from their rims. My wife still reminds me that, in those days, I had another 15 to 20 pounds of sculpted muscle in my upper body. This was very physical work, and I never thought about needing exercise. I didn't have to worry about calories, because I burned them as fast as I took them in. I didn't need to think about drinking water, because I was constantly drinking water throughout the day.

I don't know the statistics for other countries, but well over 100 million Americans today are chronically ill. Close to 70 percent of Americans 20 years of age or older are overweight or obese. One extra pound of body fat requires an additional two hundred miles of veins and arteries that must be serviced by the heart. Excessive weight is a primary factor in type 2 diabetes, coronary heart disease, high levels of LDL (bad) cholesterol, stroke, hypertension, non-alcoholic fatty liver disease, osteoarthritis, sleep apnea and other breathing problems, several forms of cancer, complications of pregnancy, and menstrual irregularities.[4]

But, how does this relate to finding the treasure inside? Our bodies were not designed to experience such inefficiencies and disease. Instead, we are made with amazing physical attributes that truly are treasures worthy of our protection. Here are just a few examples of the wonders of the human body:

You have over **twenty-five trillion red blood** cells that travel through one hundred thousand miles of veins and arteries to deliver oxygen throughout your body and pick up carbon dioxide, as if they were also trash collectors. Two to three million new red blood cells are created in your marrow every second to replace the same number that die each second. Each

---

[4] U.S. Centers for Disease Control and Prevention.

one of these microscopic red blood cells contains more than two hundred million molecules of hemoglobin.

Your nervous system includes over **three trillion nerve cells** that, lined up, would stretch some forty-five miles in length. Nerve impulses travel up to three hundred miles per hour throughout your nervous system, processing one hundred million electrochemical impulses each second.

Your **eyes are fully automatic**, self-focusing, non-blurring, motion picture cameras with one hundred twenty million photoreceptors that take instant, high-definition, three-dimensional, color pictures. In doing so, your eyes utilize one million simultaneous impressions that discriminate among nearly ten million varieties in color.

And we could go on and on. The statistics and insights into the complex eloquence of the human body are mind-boggling. Truly, as the Psalmist wrote, we are "fearfully and wonderfully made" (Psalm 139:14). The paradox is that, even though we understand more about the wonders of the human body today than ever before, we also have less physical energy and wellness than almost any other time in history. Yes, it is true that we are continually advancing our abilities to diagnose and treat illness and disease. But, on the other hand, physical energy has become a tarnished treasure, at best, for many people.

Fortunately, the way back to wellness and dynamic vitality is not complicated. With few exceptions, we can all activate this treasure inside by following these common sense and scientifically validated lifestyle practices:

Regular exercise – Any exercise is helpful. Aerobic exercise helps create cardiovascular and respiratory wellness. Most experts recommend at least three 30-minute or longer sessions of aerobic exercise per week. Regular weight bearing exercise keeps our musculo-skeletal system strong and flexible.

Plentiful amounts of purified water – Some experts say 8–10 glasses per day, others recommend drinking half our weight (pounds) in ounces each day.

Uninterrupted sleep – There is compelling scientific evidence that healthy adults need 7.5–9 hours of restful sleep every night to perform at their best physically, mentally, and emotionally. I also believe a strong case can be built that mid-day naps increase overall productivity for most adults.

Balanced, wholesome foods – The principle is quite simple: the more food you can eat that is fresh, un-packaged, and unprocessed, the higher the quality of the materials your body can utilize in maintenance and repair.

Antioxidants – This is one modern recommendation that experts universally emphasize, because of the increased presence of toxins in our environment and food supplies.

It astonishes me that, in spite of the fact that our bodies are complex beyond comprehension, these simple principles of self-care are universally potent for activating our physical energy and providing us with the best chance for long, healthy lives.

Equally incredible is the realization that, even though most people in the civilized world understand these principles, so few consistently practice them. For many years, I had the opportunity to speak globally about nutrition and wellness. One of my favorite practices was to give my audience a list of foods and lifestyle practices, both good and bad, asking them which ones were healthful and which were harmful for their personal well-being. Without fail, every audience demonstrated intelligence in knowing what was good and what was not. But I would then ask them specific questions about what they were actually doing on a regular basis. The gap between knowledge and practice was painfully evident. And, most of the time, I was speaking to people who were interested in better health!

What about you? Will you take advantage of this treasure inside? Will you activate the marvelous, self-renewing attributes in your body and optimize your physical energy? As one of my friends from the wellness industry has told me for years, "When you lose your health, nothing else matters." Or, as another has reminded me, "Ignore your health, and eventually it will go away."

Principle 18:
Faith

Before exploring the remaining principles that activate great-ness, I need to share some personal convictions with you. As with most human beings, my life journey has been a search for purpose and significance. For me, this quest led to a profound and very personal faith in God. The remaining principles that activate greatness are a direct and authentic attempt to share how my faith has shaped my respect for the treasure inside. However, you may not share a similar faith—and that is okay with me. In other words, I do not judge you for believing differently.

Several years ago, I was providing executive coaching for a very accomplished software engineer. Not only was he intelligent, but he was a wonderful human being. When we started to work on a mission statement for his career and life, he initially responded by saying, "We don't need to work on this, Ron. You see, I'm a scientist, and I don't believe in God." My response was, "I respect your position, but if you don't believe in God, we REALLY need to work on your purpose statement, because there won't be anyone else to help!"

Whether you are inclined to believe in a personal God or not, I invite you to continue this journey with me. I cannot be authentic in sharing the 23 Unexpected Principles That Activate Greatness *without including these that follow.*

F aith is taking a risk, investing your future in something and someone greater than yourself. This expression of faith is the continuous pursuit of a relationship, a communion with an invisible, yet ever-present God—as a Person. It is a personal and real connection to Him and the expression of hope and trust.

At the center of the spiritual mine is the gem of faith. The New Testament writer of Hebrews tells us that "faith is being sure of what we hope for and certain of what we do not see" (Hebrews 11:1). It is a "sixth sense," going beyond what we can comprehend with our five physical senses. It is something deeper than emotion or intellect, both a decision to trust and divine intervention in our lives.

Faith is simpler than most of us realize. I say this because I am regularly reminded of the words of Jesus to His disciples: "I tell you the truth, unless you change and become like little children, you will never enter the kingdom of heaven. Therefore, whoever humbles himself like this child is the greatest in the kingdom of heaven" (Matthew 18:3–4). Faith, then, is the simplest and most basic act—so basic, in fact, that we must become like little children to practice it properly and fully.

What did Jesus mean by "childlike"? To be like a child is to have an attitude that leads to unearthing spiritual treasures, one of humility and simple trust. This is in contrast to intellectual snobbery and pride, which seeks to impress, control, and manipulate.

Interestingly, Jesus' greatest conflicts were with religious leaders. How was it that this great spiritual giant was in almost constant conflict with the religious leaders of His time? Why didn't they recognize Him for who and what He was? More importantly, how can we keep ourselves from becoming like those religious leaders? Humility, childlike trust, a hunger to discover more of God, and a constant rejection of pride, self-serving power, and presumption make up the compass we will need for this path toward true faithfulness.

A poignant section of Eugene Peterson's *The Message* illustrates just how vital faith is to our lives:

Before you trust you have to listen. But unless Christ's Word is preached, there's nothing to listen to. [...] It's the word of faith that welcomes God to go to work and set things right for us. This is the core of our preaching. Says the welcoming word of God—"Jesus is my Master"—embracing, body and soul, God's work of doing in us what he did in raising Jesus from the dead. That's it. You're not "doing" anything; you're simply calling out to God, trusting him to do it for you. That's salvation. With your whole being you embrace God setting things right, and then you say it, right out loud: "God has set everything right between him and me!" Scripture reassures us, "No one who trusts God like this—heart and soul—will ever regret it." It's exactly the same no matter what a person's religious background may be: the same God for all of us, acting the same incredibly generous way to everyone who calls out for help. Everyone who calls, "Help, God!" gets help.

In what many have fondly called the "faith chapter," Hebrews 11 teaches us that "without faith it is impossible to please God, because anyone who comes to Him must believe that He exists and that He rewards those who earnestly seek Him." James, the senior leader of the first Christian church in Jerusalem reinforces this by stating, "If any of you lacks wisdom, he should ask God, who gives generously to all without finding fault, and it will be given to him. But when he asks, he must believe and not doubt, because he who doubts is like a wave of the sea, blown and tossed by the wind" (James 1:5–6). This passage is such a powerful statement about the treasure of faith! How can any of us claim a lack of wisdom as an excuse, when we are encouraged that God gives generously to all without finding fault?

My initial steps of faith were completely ignorant and timid. I hungered to know if God was real and, if He was, what that should mean to me. I explored several religious and secular philosophies, hoping to find purpose and context for my life. I wanted to discover faith in my own way, but I continually found myself trapped in my own intellect and emotions. My hunger was satisfied intermittently, but, somewhere deeper in my soul, I knew it couldn't be real unless it was something bigger than me. If God was real, He couldn't just be a creation of my imagination. I wanted to be arrested by some great spiritual experience, to be confronted with some physical manifestation of the reality of God. It wasn't until I became as a little child that I discovered this treasure. And, it was so simple that I wasn't even aware of the power of faith when it first awakened me. I have found that my experience wasn't entirely unique. For many people, the initial steps into faith can be confusing, uncertain, and filled with questions as we attempt to discover genuine spirituality.

One night, Jesus was visited by one of the leaders of the Jewish ruling council, Nicodemus. Let's listen in on their conversation (adapted from John 3):

Nicodemus: We know you are a teacher who has come from God. No one could perform the miracles we have seen you perform if God wasn't with him.

Jesus: Let me give you the truth, Nicodemus: No one can see the kingdom of God unless he goes through a rebirth.

Nicodemus: I don't understand. [He understood more than he was letting on.] Can a person be reborn when he is old? You can't be talking about a person jumping back into his mother's womb?

Jesus: I will pretend I didn't hear you say that. Let me give you the truth you are seeking again: No one can enter the kingdom of God unless he is born both by his mother and by the Spirit, who is above. Sure, you have been born of the flesh, but you also have to be born of the Spirit. This shouldn't surprise you, Nicodemus. It is much like the wind—you can't actually see it, but you see its effect. It seems to blow wherever it wants, and you really don't know where it is going to go next. It is the same way with anyone being born of the Spirit.

Nicodemus: How can this be? This doesn't seem to fit with our traditions.

Jesus: Here you are, a religious teacher, and you can't understand this simple concept of the beginning of spiritual life? Believe me, Nicodemus, I know what I'm talking about, and yet you still can't accept what I'm saying. Remember, you started this conversation by saying that you know I am from God because of the miracles you have watched me perform. I'm just scratching the surface by putting it in a context you can readily understand, and yet you still can't accept it. What if I started telling you things about heaven that can't even be compared with anything here on earth—what would you say then? Let's try just a little: No one has ever gone into heaven up to this point, except for me and that is because I came from heaven! How does that fit with your religious tradition?

Do you remember the story of the Israelites rebelling against Moses and God in the desert and being attacked by venomous snakes? Remember what God told Moses to do in order to save the people? He instructed Moses to make a bronze snake and put it on a pole in front of the people. Whoever looked at the bronze snake survived, and those who refused to look at the snake on the pole died. Think about that story and, one day, you will figure out who I am.

The truth is, Nicodemus, that God loved the world so much that He sent me, so that whoever believes in me will never die, but will be born of the Spirit and will enjoy life forever. He didn't send me here to condemn everybody—instead, He sent me so that everyone who believes in me could escape condemnation and be saved from misery and destruction. Whoever chooses to believe in me is already guaranteed life, but if you choose to not believe in me, you bring condemnation on yourself.

So, this is the final conclusion of our discussion, Nicodemus, since you are seeking the truth: Spiritual light has come into the world, but people prefer darkness instead of light, because so many of their past actions have been wrong. Everyone who does bad things hates the light because it exposes them for who they really are. But, if you are really seeking the truth, you will come into the light, and the light itself will show that you have chosen to do the will of God.

True spiritual treasures confront, challenge, and change us. They don't help us justify or rationalize our current condition; instead, they offer a way out through the love, dependability, and wisdom of a God bigger than our imagination or religious tradition. In my own journey, it wasn't until I faced my imperfections and failures that I stumbled into a revelation: I needed to be born of the Spirit.

My spiritual breakthrough came when I prayed the following:

> God, I know You are real and I realize that I cannot make any demands on You because I have failed in so many different ways. I know I have failed myself, so I must have failed You even more, in ways that I'm not even aware of right now. I guess the only chance I have to know You and be accepted by You is to ask for Your forgiveness and accept that Jesus died for my sins. Please help me to understand and to hear Your voice in my spirit. I don't know how yet, but I want to give my life to You, and I want to learn to hear You and obey You, so that I can fulfill Your purpose for my life. Thank You for accepting me, even while I'm at my worst, and thank You for taking charge of my life from this point on. In Jesus' name, Amen.

That prayer wasn't deep or very enlightened. But, because it was the pathway God created for anyone to begin a relationship with Him, it worked. For more than forty years, I have continued that adventure, and I can say with total confidence, "No one who trusts God like this—heart and soul—will ever regret it."

"Unbelief is abnormal; belief is normal. For the normal human being will joyfully embrace faith and belief, but the cynical doubter cannot believe and will not believe until he can be healed of the negative memories that plague him and block him from his innate ability to see God."

— Robert H. Schuller, *The Be (Happy) Attitudes*

Principle 19:
Prayer

Prayer is so simple;
It is like quietly opening a door
And slipping into the very presence of God,
There in the stillness
To listen to His voice;
Perhaps to petition,
Or only to listen;
It matters not.
Just to be there
In His presence
Is prayer.

— Author Unknown

Prayer is mysterious, inexplicable, and personal. Nonetheless, people all over the world, of many faiths and traditions, fully believe in and practice the discipline of prayer.

Prayer was a vital part of Jesus' life on earth. Scripture reveals that Jesus often rose early before sunrise and went out alone to pray. How is it that He, who was supposed to be the incarnation of God, still needed to pray? Through becoming the Son of Man, did He intentionally limit His connection to the Father to what was available to humankind—prayer? His followers asked Him to teach them how to pray. Most people raised in a Christian culture are familiar with the prayer He taught; it provides a simple, but comprehensive, model for prayer. Let's look at Eugene Peterson's adaptation of this prayer in Matthew 6:9–13 of *The Message*:

> Our Father in heaven,
> Reveal who you are.
> Set the world right:
> Do what's best—as above, so below.
> Keep us alive with three square meals.
> Keep us forgiven with you and forgiving others.
> Keep us safe from ourselves and the Devil.
> You're in charge!
> You can do anything you want!
> You're ablaze in beauty!
> Yes. Yes. Yes.

If we follow this model of prayer, and all that the Bible teaches about prayer is true, why is it that some prayers just don't seem to get answered? Some qualifiers are given throughout the Bible to help us understand the imperfect nature of this exploration of prayer. First, Jesus taught that prayer must be persistent. To capture the original language (Greek) of the Book of Luke, Jesus told His disciples to "ask and keep on asking, and it shall be given to you; seek and keep on seeking, and you shall find; knock and keep on knocking, and the door shall be opened" (Luke 11:9, *The Amplified Bible*). I believe that the most common reason for unanswered prayer is a lack of persistence. A great example of this is found in Luke 18:1–8, which has been re-interpreted here in *The Message*:

> Jesus told them a story showing that it was necessary for them to pray consistently and never quit. He said, "There was once a judge in some city who never gave God a thought and cared nothing for people. A widow in that city kept after him: 'My rights are being violated. Protect me!' He never gave her the time of day. But after this went on and on he said to himself, 'I care nothing what God thinks, even less what people think. But because this widow won't quit badgering me, I'd better do something and see that she gets justice—otherwise I'm going to end up beaten black-and-blue by her pounding.'" Then the Master said, "Do you hear what that judge, corrupt as he is, is saying? So what makes you think God won't step in and work justice for his chosen people, who continue to cry out for help? Won't he stick up for them? I assure you, he will. He will not drag his feet. But how much of that kind of persistent faith will the Son of Man find on the earth when he returns?"

Another reason for unanswered prayer, revealed in Scripture, is praying with the wrong motives. James wrote in his New Testament letter, "You do not have because you do not ask God. When you ask, you do not receive, because you ask with wrong motives, that you may spend what you get on your pleasures" (James 4:2–3).

And, finally, sometimes our prayers aren't answered because they conflict with the purpose of God in our lives. In Gethsemane, as Jesus prepared for His suffering, He prayed, "My Father, if it is possible, may this cup be taken from me. Yet not as I will, but as you will" (Matthew 26:39). It may seem cruel for God to not have answered Jesus' prayer. But, as painful as life can be, God has a perspective rooted in eternity that recognizes the purpose and brevity of suffering during this life. If we can reach out in faith, there are treasures to be found in suffering that are too precious and mysterious to understand apart from divine illumination. Besides, there is so much to come in heaven.

At its very core, prayer is simply cultivating and enjoying a relationship with God. We learn from the example and instructions of Jesus, and we grow in this relationship just as our faith grows—one day at a time. One of the most powerful prayer exercises I have discovered is the practice of writing out my prayers as a two-way conversation with God. Here is an example:

Ron: Good morning, Lord.

Lord: Good morning, Ron.

Ron: I love You, Lord. Thank You for adopting me into Your family. Thank You for cleansing me of all of the mistakes I have made. Thank You for giving me this opportunity to spend time with You today.

Lord: You're welcome, Ron. I love you, and I want to show you more of Myself today. Come close to Me in faith. Open up your heart to Me, and I will speak words of encouragement to you.

I use my laptop to capture these times of fellowship together, and they have increased my faith tremendously. Of course, I don't consider these prayer logs to be infallible, nor do I consider myself to be a perfect listener—these written conversations are simply an experiment to help me grow in my spiritual receptivity. Over time, they have helped to open up my spiritual ears to enjoy a more intimate relationship with God.

How about you? Would you like to have a daily appointment with the Creator of the universe? If it were possible, would you want to develop an intimate, unique relationship with God Almighty? Would you consider that a treasure worth pursuing? If so, He is waiting for you to come on in—through prayer.

> **"Prayer is not overcrowding God's reluctance,**
> **but taking hold of God's willingness."**
> **— Anonymous**

Principle 20:

Transformation

Last night my little boy confessed to me some
childish wrong;
And kneeling at my knee he prayed with tears—
"Dear God, make me a man like Daddy—wise and strong.
I know you can."
Then while he slept I knelt beside his bed, confessed
my sins, and prayed with low-bowed head,
"O God, make me a child like my child here—
pure, guileless, trusting Thee with faith sincere."

— Author Unknown

On August 4, 1971, I made an inner decision to turn away from "salvation by self-help" and welcome the power of confession and repentance into my life. At approximately 2:00 in the morning, I prayed something similar to what is known as "the sinner's prayer." During that prayer, I asked God for forgiveness and rebirth into the family of God; this simple act of confession, and subsequent repentance, changed my life. But, it was not a once-for-all-time event. It was the beginning of a new way of living, the recognition that I needed to turn toward God and set aside my ways to pursue His ways. Since that day, confession and repentance have helped me find a tangible change in direction, allowing me to explore spiritual treasures over and over again. Together, they are the key to remaining teachable, flexible, and changeable as I seek to continually experience the presence of God— and, thereby, become more like Him.

Confession, the first part of transformation, is hard to quantify, explain, or describe; it's not merely a ritual, a group conversion, or the result of an intense interrogation. The prophet Isaiah wrote: "Seek the LORD while He may be found; call on Him while He is near. Let the wicked forsake his way and the evil man his thoughts. Let him turn to the Lord, and He will have mercy on him, and to our God, for He will freely pardon." (Isaiah 55:6–7). In the original language of the New Testament, confession literally means, "saying the same as." In other words, in a spiritual context, it is "to agree with God." An important implication in this definition is that confession is spoken out loud, as opposed to silent prayer or meditation (which each have their own value). To recognize the potential power in confession, let's look at what the apostle Paul says in his letter to the Church of Rome:

> "The word is near you; it is in your mouth and in your heart," that is, the word of faith we are proclaim- ing: That if you confess with your mouth, "Jesus is

Lord," and believe in your heart that God raised Him from the dead, you will be saved. For it is with your heart that you believe and are justified, and it is with your mouth that you confess and are saved. (Romans 10:8-10)

In this passage, we can clearly see that confession is by no means limited to admission of guilt, but is, rather, a process of agreeing with God first in our hearts and then with our tongues. Jesus said, "For out of the overflow of the heart the mouth speaks. [...] For by your words you will be acquitted, and by your words you will be condemned." (Matthew 12:34, 37). To be forgiven, then, we must confess our sins verbally. Confession, according to Biblical teaching, is similar to, but distinct from, everyday prayer.

In addition to speaking out loud, in order to fully experience confession's power, we must address both the nature of our sin and the experience with that sin, as well as the righteousness of God's love. This may seem awkward and difficult at first, but it can become a source of great strength and transformation when made a regular part of our daily lives. And, as we discover the power that confession has in our own lives, we can use this power to bless the lives of those around us.

So, how can confession of sin release goodness into our lives? Confession is a source of great treasure, because recognition of the truth brings freedom. When we agree with God's definition of sin, we align ourselves with reality. By confessing our sins, we free ourselves from the burden of guilt, alienation, and estrangement from a pure and holy God. We return to the naked truth that we are all sinners and rebellious by nature, afflicted by an inherited flaw that cannot be overcome by our own efforts, regardless of how noble they may be. In acknowledging our failure through confession, we position ourselves to receive God's divine intervention and, in doing so, also embrace the powerful treasure of repentance. We are refreshed by the mercies of God, which Scripture tells us are renewed every morning throughout our lives.

Through confession, we also allow ourselves to be fully transformed. Consider God's perspective from 2 Corinthians 5:17: "Therefore, if anyone is in Christ, he is a new creation; the old has gone, the new has come!" Imagine what a transformation would occur if you truly believed and regularly confessed these "God perspectives" about yourself! Think of the transformational impact it could have on your relationships if you were able to start viewing those around you as recipients of this destiny from God.

If confession is the act of verbalizing our sins and becoming clean through Christ, then repentance is the catalyst for change. Interestingly, a common misconception is that repentance means to show great remorse or emotion. By combining the languages of the Old and New Testaments, however, repentance can be described as an inner change of mind that results in an outward change of direction.

A great example of the concept of repentance is found in the admonition to "forgive those who trespass against us."

The Bible, as well as almost every other sacred religious text, contains strong exhortations to forgive those who commit an injustice against us. Yet, resentment, combined with an unforgiving spirit, is probably the single greatest cause of estrangement and emotional suffering today, often expanding its tentacles beyond our emotional well-being, poisoning our spiritual and physical health as well.

It is easy to talk of forgiveness in theoretical terms or see the damage resentment wreaks in the lives of those around us. However, it can be quite a different matter when the resentment resides within us. The Scriptures are so clear about the devastating effect an unforgiving attitude has on our lives— there is no logical rationalization to hold on to resentment. At the same time, forgiveness is one of the hardest spiritual disciplines to consistently practice. That's why we need repentance. By recognizing the destructive nature of resentment, we can make an inner decision to change our minds about the offending persons. Then, we can complete repentance by turning away from resentment and taking some action that expresses our turning toward God and extending forgiveness.

Sometimes, this act of repentance will need to be repeated over and over again to achieve complete freedom. In Eugene Peterson's *The Message*, we read that, "Peter got up the nerve to ask, 'Master, how many times do I forgive a brother or sister who hurts me? Seven?' Jesus replied, 'Seven! Hardly. Try seventy times seven.'" (Matthew 18:21–22). Forgiveness doesn't have a limit with God; if we are trying to emulate Him, then we should try to extend forgiveness in limitless quantities, too.

Another tremendous example of the power of repentance and forgiveness is the story of Corrie Ten Boom, author of *The Hiding Place*. Corrie was a young, Lutheran girl from Denmark whose family hid Jewish people in their attic during World War II. When they were discovered, they were shipped off to death camps, and Corrie watched her sister suffer at the hands of a particularly cruel guard. Years later, in a church service, a man came up to Corrie and introduced himself; he was the guard responsible for her dear sister's death. With every fiber in her body wanting revenge, Corrie found the power of repentance and, against all human emotion, extended her love and forgiveness to this man, who had since become a part of the family of God. Could you do the same?

Yet another example of the power of repentance can be discovered as we navigate the battles and challenges of daily life. We live in an imperfect world, and we are still going through the process of transformation. Some days, we experience tremendous advances; other days, it seems as though everything we have been seeking to accomplish in our spiritual journey falls apart. There are times of great victory over temptation and, sooner or later, there will be times when we falter and succumb. Whether these failures are great or small, confession and repentance always gives us a road back. We begin by confessing our sins and making an inner decision to change, followed by an outward turning away from our waywardness, back toward God's mercy and grace. There is a song I regularly sing as a reminder of how easy it is to turn back and return to God's favor:

> The steadfast love of the Lord never ceases,
> His mercies never come to an end.
> They are new every morning, new every morning,
> Great is thy faithfulness, O Lord, great is thy faithfulness.
> (adapted from Lamentations 3:22–23, KJV)

If we begin to view ourselves from God's perspective and make this song a part of our regular confession, we effectively invite the presence of God deeper and deeper into our lives. As we agree with Him through confession, and fully experience repentance, we begin to take on His likeness and, over time, achieve the very thing we had hoped to achieve before through self-effort: to become like God. In the process, we become partakers of divine nature, not through the worn-out attempts of self-effort, but as a result of the empowering presence of God. By agreeing with God and understanding confession, then changing our actions through repentance, we discover an immeasurable treasure that can never be depleted or exhausted of its wealth.

"If we claim to be without sin, we deceive ourselves and the truth is not in us. If we confess our sins, He is faithful and just and will forgive us our sins and purify us from all unrighteousness." (1 John 1:8–9).

Principle 21:
Relationship

"Worship is a deliberate and disciplined
adventure in reality."
— Willard Sperry, author

Just as we were made to eat, drink, breathe, move, sleep, and love, we were made to worship. Something deep in all of us longs to worship, adore, and revere. It will—it must—find expression in our lives. Some of us choose to worship nature or the arts, while others "deify" a person. Some people worship past spiritual or national leaders, ancestors, or a broad assortment of "gods." And some of us are bold enough to worship ourselves, thinking that we are ascending into divinity through education, enlightenment, and self-development. We all express worship in one way or another—it is a part of us.

So, how can worship be considered a spiritual treasure? Worship comes from within us, rather than from some other source. It is a treasure that can open up the unimaginable opportunity to share an intimate relationship with the Creator of the universe. Think about that for a moment—intimacy with the Creator of the universe! And, to top it off, worship brings additional goodness to our lives. Let's look at this in depth:

First, intimate worship gives us a more accurate perspective of reality. Worship helps to lift us out of our self-centeredness and gives us a glimpse of the true reality, that all of creation is centered on its Creator.

Second, worship creates opportunities for divine intervention (or divine invasion). As a result of worship, we become more aware of God's purpose and presence. We develop new sensitivities so that we recognize Him in situations that we previously took credit for or blamed on others. Worship helps us realize that God is the ultimate macro- and micromanager—He holds everything together, while taking a genuine interest in the minutest of details.

Third, worship changes us. Worship helps us to realize how far we fall short of God's character, wisdom, and righteousness, while at the same time drawing us into a personal revelation of how wonderful and all-encompassing His love and provision for us is. It is both scary and sacred at the same time. Our times of worship in God's presence will create a noticeable change in who and what we are.

Are you beginning to see how worship can be a wonderful, life-changing intimacy with God? With this in mind, there is a pattern of worship that helps us enter into God's presence.

These seven steps into worship are not intended to form a new ritual. Instead, they help us to move away from self-consciousness and into God-consciousness as we go on a "date with God." These steps are:

1. Give thanks. Begin by thanking God for every good thing in your life, then start giving thanks for the difficulties and disappointments also, because He works all things for your good. Examples of thanksgiving are found in Psalm 100, Psalm 107, 1 Chronicles 16:8–12, 1 Thessalonians 5:16–18, and 1 Chronicles 29:10–19.

2. Praise God. Transition from thanksgiving to praising God for who He is. Praise is an expression of approval, esteem, or commendation and can be shown in many creative ways. Examples of praise are found in 1 Chronicles 16:8–36 and Psalm 8, 34, 47, 103, 145, and 150.

3. Worship Him. Move from praise into deeper adoration, reverence, and expression of your love. The primary goal of worship, at this point, is to relate directly and intimately with God as a Person. Examples of worship are found in Exodus 33:5–8, 2 Chronicles 7:1–3, Psalm 63, and Revelation 4:6–11.

4. Be silent. As you begin to experience God's presence (through His Spirit), there will be times when you recognize Him taking the initiative and speaking to your heart. Learning to wait on God and practicing what author Dr. Mary Ruth Swope refers to as "Listening Prayer" will enrich your experience and release the artesian well inside of you that gushes fountains of life (see Psalm 27:14 and 46:10).

5. Record your experience. You can commemorate your experiences by writing them down, so take some time toward the end of your "date with God" to journal about what you experienced. If you do this while continuing to enjoy God's presence, your journaling will grow into an extension of your relationship and new insights will come to you as you write.

6. Enjoy the afterglow. As you move toward the end of your time of worship, continue to express praise and thanksgiving. Back out of the presence of the King, rather than turning your back on Him by promptly ceasing worship. The more respect and reverence you demonstrate, the higher the quality of your relationship will become.

7. Go and obey. Inevitably, your worship experiences will generate new inspirations for actions to take in your life. Imagine coming back into God's presence and being able to report to Him that you have completed the actions He gave you the last time you had fellowship together.

This pattern helps you to focus your relationship with God and unlocks continuous treasures of wisdom, strength, comfort, and renewal. However, worship can enhance your life far beyond special times that you set aside to have a date with God.

All of this is very much like my relationship with my wife. We are together every day, going about the many responsibilities of life. However, for our relationship to remain vibrant, we also need special times to be together, to focus on our relationship and intimate fellowship with one another, instead of the tasks that continually demand our attention. We pursue these special times through a dinner out, a vacation away from the rest of our family, or by simply taking a walk together.

Just like a marital relationship, focused time with God (worship) allows you to grow closer to Him. So, too, worship should be both a continual recognition of God's presence and friendship in your life, along with special times of worship when you can focus specifically on your relationship with one another. How can your life be enhanced by worship? There's no need to wait to find out—the opportunity is available to you, right here and now.

"One who knows God, worships God."

— Anonymous

Principle 22:

Gratitude

"He who is thankful for little, enjoys much."

— Anonymous

I recently realized that there is only one national holiday named after an attitude: Thanksgiving. Although Canadians celebrate it the second Monday in October and Americans celebrate it the fourth Thursday in November, the idea behind it is the same. When we were kids, Thanksgiving meant lots of food and a day of fun with cousins, aunts, uncles, grandparents, and the occasional family acquaintance that had nowhere else to celebrate. It's a time to enjoy the company of loved ones—like Christmas, but without the gifts.

As children, we learned that the holiday was about more than just getting together for a big meal. We were told the story of the Pilgrims who sailed to Plymouth Rock in Cape Cod in 1620. The Pilgrims' first Thanksgiving dinner was established to give thanks for their survival and to extend friendship to the local Wampanoag Indians. But, one has to wonder, to give thanks for what? In their first year, the Pilgrims lost forty-seven of the ninety-nine passengers due to illness and the harsh conditions at sea. All but three families lost loved ones, and thirteen of the eighteen mothers who crossed the Atlantic died. In spite of this seemingly unbearable suffering, they gathered to give thanks.

What strength of character it must have taken to be thankful in the midst of so much suffering. In order for us to be thankful today, most of us need our thermostat adjusted just right, our refrigerator full, and our favorite television program on. And, of course, the kids need to be quiet! Yet, these Pilgrims, with so few possessions and so much suffering, gathered to give thanks for the providence that brought them through their first winter in the New World.

Take a moment to reflect on your interactions over the last several days. Think about your last conversation with a friend, coworker, or family member. What did you talk about? What did the other person say? In watching the way people interact with one another, I have discovered something very interesting: quite often, people spend a good amount of time complaining. In contrast, I have also noticed that people prefer to be around someone who is grateful more than someone who is complaining. Furthermore, I have observed that most people are starved for some genuine appreciation. And, I have discovered that I change internally when I cultivate a habit of giving thanks at every opportunity.

It is almost impossible to be thankful and complaining at the same time—one or the other has to go. So, if you focus on genuine gratitude, much of the misery of life disappears. When you fill your mind up with thanksgiving, it's not comfortable hanging around someone with a critical and negative attitude. I have also noticed that almost every problem begins to shrink in size when my life is permeated with a grateful attitude.

So, why aren't more of us thankful? Because it isn't easy. By nature, we find it easier to focus on the seemingly greener grass on the other side of the fence, blame circumstances and other people for our unhappiness and disappointments, and attempt to boost our own self-esteem by finding faults in others. We may attempt to find happiness by changing friends, commitments, and locations, only to find that it takes just a short time for misery to return—because we bring it with us!

Pride can also cause a lack of thankfulness. As H.W. Beecher said, "A proud man is seldom a grateful man, for he never thinks he gets as much as he deserves." The connection between pride and ingratitude is profound. Can we assume that, whenever we succumb to whining, we are also exposing an unhealthy pride? And, can we further conclude that one of the greatest weapons we have against ugly pride is thankfulness? I think so—and there are many promises in the Scriptures for the humble woman or man:

> When pride comes, then comes disgrace, but with humility comes wisdom. (Proverbs 11:2)

> Humility and the fear of the LORD bring wealth and honor and life. (Proverbs 22:4)

141

All of you, clothe yourselves with humility toward one another, because, "God opposes the proud but gives grace to the humble." Humble yourselves, therefore, under God's mighty hand, that he may lift you up in due time. (1 Peter 5:5–6)

I have spoken and written about thanksgiving many times over the years. Yet, it was in the writing of this chapter that I saw, for the first time, the direct connection between thankfulness, humility, and the fear of God. In counseling sessions, people often acknowledge pride and reckless living, asking for guidance about how to change what seem to be unbreakable patterns. The answer is easy: give thanks. If they are anything, pride and reckless living are the fruit of ingratitude and, therefore, irresponsible living.

Here are some ideas on how to make thankfulness a habit:

Spend at least thirty minutes making a list of everything you own. You probably won't capture everything in thirty minutes, but you will realize how much you have— and how much you have to be thankful for. And, you will also have a detailed list to use when giving thanks.

Spend at least thirty minutes making a list of everyone you know. Again, you will probably not get everyone on the list in thirty minutes. Writing their names down, however, will help you see how much love, friendship, and support you actually have. Keep this list for times when you are feeling lonely, and it will help you realize the great number of people in your life.

Spend at least thirty minutes making a list of every talent or ability you have. List everything, not just the big things like painting or music. Most of us will finish this exercise early because we suffer from low self-esteem—I encourage you to push past this feeling. This list will give you much to be thankful for (as well as boost your confidence level).

By completing these exercises, you will activate the principle of gratitude. Remember: thanksgiving can change your life, attitude, and situation—without actually changing a thing.

> Think of the hopes that lie before you,
> Not the waste that lies behind;
> Think of the treasures you have gathered,
> Not the ones you've failed to find;
> Think of the service you may render,
> Not of serving self alone;
> Think of the happiness of others,
> And in this you'll find your own!
>
> — Robert E. Farley

Principle 23:
Giving

P ower. The word alone evokes a sense of awe. It is a resource that allows us to better our current condition, giving us the opportunity to break out of our current state and activate the treasure inside.

These many pages have been centered on finding, unearthing, and utilizing sources of personal power. As we've discovered, life-changing inner resources are universally available, yet mysteriously dormant. In many ways, our inner resources are similar to unpolished diamonds—they appear plain, common, and of minimal value at first glance. But, as we learned from Al Hafed's tragedy, these seemingly worthless rocks can be cut and polished to expose brilliant gems within.

Most people are in the habit of attributing power to circumstances, others, and fate. We fall short of our hopes and abandon our dreams, blaming the economy, the government, painful and dysfunctional childhoods, and abuse from teachers and employers. Sometimes, we shrug our shoulders, blaming these life changes on aging. Our sense of purpose and control is easily lost, but our inner treasures still remain, crying out from deep within, that we might discover and employ them for a brighter, more dynamic, and more fulfilling future.

Good things will only come from taking ownership of your fate. Success, prosperity, fulfillment, and happiness don't come from the latest business opportunity, a rich uncle, or a winning lottery ticket. The highest and noblest results in life always come from tapping into these resources of hidden treasures and releasing the latent power within.

I would like to share one more principle I have discovered that is inseparable from lasting achievement and fulfillment. This final activating principle, available to all of us, is the privilege of giving.

John D. Rockefeller, one of the wealthiest men in American history, spent a good portion of his life getting and accumulating. He was known as a tough, sometimes ruthless, businessman. Yet, his accumulation of wealth, political power, and reputation didn't bring peace or contentment. In his later years, he discovered the truth in Henry Drummond's statement that real happiness is in giving, rather than getting. He made giving his number-one priority, and the Rockefeller Foundation continues to be one of the most generous philanthropic organizations today, more than

seven decades after his death. I believe that John D. Rockefeller has been much maligned by those who have written about him; not understanding the depth of his conversion, they accused him of giving to relieve a guilty conscience. However, a closer and more discerning investigation reveals a man who discovered one of the greatest secrets of life: the power of giving!

The Scriptures also have plenty to say about giving:

Honor the LORD from your wealth, with the first-fruits of all your crops; then your barns will be filled to overflowing, and your vats will brim over with new wine. (Proverbs 3:9–10)

He who gives to the poor will lack nothing, but he who closes his eyes to them receives many curses. (Proverbs 28:27)

Give, and it will be given unto you. A good measure, pressed down, shaken together and running over, will be poured into your lap. For with the measure you use, it will be measured to you. (Luke 6:38)

Remember this: Whoever sows sparingly will also reap sparingly, and whoever sows generously will also reap generously. Each man should give what he has decided in his heart to give, not reluctantly or under compulsion, for God loves a cheerful giver. (2 Corinthians 9:6–7)

Here are some suggestions for releasing the full power of giving into your life:

Give early and give often. No matter where you find yourself today, find some way to give. Don't worry about how much or how little; just start giving. Longfellow wrote, "Give what you have. To someone, it may be better than you dare to think." But, be sure to give without going into debt, for most of the joy in giving is lost when it results in a credit card bill you can't pay the next month. If money is lacking, you can give time, energy, emotional support, and material possessions. Giving early and often opens you up to the goodness that will come to you as a result of generosity.

Give to those who cannot give in return. One of the great promises in the Bible is that he who gives to the poor gives to his Maker. John Wesley wrote, "The more good we do, the happier we shall be. The more we deal our bread to the hungry, and cover the naked with garments; the more we relieve the stranger, and visit them that are sick or in prison; the more kind offices we do to those that groan under the various evils of human life, the more comfort we receive even in the present world; the greater the recompense we have in our own bosom." Giving to those who cannot give in return is a key to activating the principle of giving in your life.

Give to those who oppose you. This is, understandably, one of the most difficult giving disciplines. But, it may have more inherent power than any other kind of giving in life.

When we learn generosity with our enemies, we develop a depth of giving that reflects the Divine. The apostle Paul captured the essence of the ultimate gift when he wrote, "God demonstrates His own love for us in this: While we were still sinners, Christ died for us" (Romans 5:8). In Jesus' famous Sermon on the Mount—which I believe is one of the all-time greatest treatises on personal power—He told His followers, "You have heard that it was said, 'Love your neighbor and hate your enemy.' But I tell you: Love your enemies and pray for those who persecute you, that you may be sons of your Father in heaven." (Matthew 5:43–45). When we can cheerfully give to those who oppose us, the kingdom of heaven is not far away.

Giving is an attitude. When you give freely, goodness will begin to come to you in greater and greater quantities. It only takes an open heart and a willingness to give. And, with those two things, all of the good that is inside will be set free in the joy of giving.

> "A committed giver is an incurably happy person,
> a secure person, a satisfied person,
> and a prosperous person."
> — Eric Butterworth

.

Epliogue

A writer asked George Bernard Shaw to play the "what if" game shortly before he died.

"Mr. Shaw," he said, "you have visited with some of the most famous people in the world. You have known royalty, world-renowned authors, artists, teachers, and dignitaries from every part of the world. If you could live your life over and be anybody you have known, or any person from history, who would you choose to be?"

Shaw replied, "I would choose to be the man George Bernard Shaw could have been, but never was."

Pursuing your potential is not found in attempting to be like someone else or achieving what someone else has achieved. It is a pursuit of the available reservoirs of potential within you. Sadly, few people come anywhere close to exhausting these resources within.

You have now been introduced to the 23 unexpected principles that activate greatness. Some folks may conclude, "These aren't all that surprising. Most of these ideas have been around for hundreds, if not thousands, of years." This is true. However, what makes them surprising is that they have always been within your grasp. The question to ask yourself is, "How much am I using these principles to activate my treasure within?"

At some point in life, each of us aspires to greatness. Not a greatness defined by others, but a purpose that each of us feels deep within. Something or someone impacts us in a way that makes us respond, "I want to be _____" or "I want to achieve _____ before my life is over." For some, it is triggered by a role model who inspires us early in life. For others, it is a reaction to a negative experience or relationship that has shown us the dark side of life. In either case, the key to greatness is how we respond to our aspirations.

Unfortunately, far too many people trade this hunger for greatness for a more secure, predictable existence of mediocrity and self-protection. Many of us surrender our dreams because of personal failure. We disappoint ourselves and lose confidence. Some of us walk away from our dreams because of perceived obligations to others. Still others of us lose faith because of cynicism from the inevitable setbacks and disappointments we encounter along the way. Yet, if you listen to your heart—really listen deeply—this yearning for greatness can still be heard, because it is a part of life itself.

It doesn't matter how many years have passed since you first experienced this pull toward greatness. It still lives as a treasure inside, waiting for you to activate its power, using one or several of the principles we have explored together. This treasure lives in you because it is a gift from God. It makes you much more important in the lives of others than you probably understand.

Your treasure inside is timeless. It doesn't matter what your age is, where you have already been, or the extent of success or failure you have experienced up to this point. The past cannot be changed, whether good or bad. Today is the day for you to activate these 23 principles in your life in pursuit of your fullest potential. The choices you make to practice these principles will unleash how much greatness you share with the world tomorrow.

I wish you all the best as you release your treasure inside.

Self-Assessment for the Treasure Inside 23 Principles

Read through and check the accurate statements under each of the 23 Principles listed below. Review your responses and choose 1 – 3 principles to focus on for personal development over the next 30, 60, or 90 days. Develop an action plan based on this and set a future appointment with yourself to review your progress and repeat the process again. For added benefit, share your focus and action plan with a trusted friend.

For more ideas on how to activate these principles, see www.TreasureInsideBook.com

Principle 1: Diamonds
- ☐ I consistently look for hidden potential in my current circumstances.
- ☐ I recognize and resist the temptation to believe that the grass is greener on the other side of the fence.

Principle 2: Pressure
- ☐ I welcome the pressures I experience day-to-day, because I recognize the refining impact they have on who I am becoming.
- ☐ I am able to recognize several facets of difficult experiences, both good and bad.

Principle 3: Optimism
- ☐ I have accepted responsibility for managing my thoughts, realizing that I move toward what I think about day-to-day.

☐ I intentionally limit my exposure to negative thinking patterns in relationships, the media, and online.

☐ I have written an exciting description of who I want to become in the future, and I refer to it at least once every week.

☐ I have written lifetime goals for what I want to achieve, and I refer to them at least once a month.

☐ Overall, I believe I am optimistic about my future potential, and I am committed to pursuing it.

Principle 4: Possibilities

☐ I have reflected and written in a journal within the past twelve months about what my potential is in the future.

☐ I consistently set aside time each week with the specific purpose of pursuing my future potential.

☐ I invest my own money each year in professional development, and my investment is proportionate to the goal of optimizing my potential.

☐ I have written affirmations that reflect who I am as my "better self," and I repeat these daily.

☐ I regularly put myself into challenging or stretching situations to accelerate my learning.

Principle 5: Refinement

☐ Most days, I read at least 30 minutes from books that help develop me professionally and personally.

☐ I outline or summarize the books I read at least 50 percent of the time.

- ☐ I set new professional development goals or create new action plans based on the books I read.
- ☐ I have read at least five books on professional development over the past 12 months.
- ☐ I have given away at least ten books (single or multiple titles) to others over the past 12 months because of the impact these books had on my life.

Principle 6: Choices

- ☐ I can think of at least three significant choices I made in the past that changed the course of my life for the better.
- ☐ Most of the time, when confronted with failure or disappointment, I choose to focus on what I can control instead of losing energy worrying about or resenting what I cannot control.
- ☐ I can think of three specific choices I am intentionally implementing right now that cut against the grain of just following the path of least resistance.
- ☐ I am consistently conscious of what attitudes will empower me to do the most good in my life.
- ☐ I have a thoughtful, written blueprint for the thoughts, attitudes, and actions that will empower me, regardless of my situation.

Principle 7: Visualization

- ☐ I have written a vision of who I want to become and what I want to achieve in the next ten years (or longer).

- [ ] I have a system and am able to devote part of my energy every day to my most important goals, even if they are not urgent.
- [ ] I have been consciously aligning my thoughts, attitudes, and actions around a clearly defined vision of the future for the last 12 months (or longer).
- [ ] I have a plan for what I need to do over the next 6–12 months to keep moving in the direction of my vision.

Principle 8: Intention

- [ ] I have a list of financial, physical, intellectual, social, and/or spiritual goals for the next 3–5 years.
- [ ] My goals are consistently SMART (specific, measureable, achievable, relevant, and time bound) and written.
- [ ] I have written intermediate goals for the next 3–12 months, and I refer to them at least once a month.
- [ ] I set monthly goals that I have an 80 percent chance or better of achieving, and I consistently record my results.
- [ ] I share my goals with at least one other person who can encourage and challenge me.

Principle 9: Providence

- [ ] I consistently make and keep commitments to myself.
- [ ] I am not afraid to make big commitments that will change my future.
- [ ] Once I have made a commitment, I am tenacious and will not accept excuses, only results.

☐ Once I have made a commitment, I expect and look for Providence to help.

Principle 10: Intensity

☐ My current level of desire to push for my optimal potential is higher than a "7" on a scale of 1–10 (with 10 being the highest).

☐ I have a written life mission or purpose statement that energizes me whenever I take time to reflect on it.

☐ I regularly go to bed with a good fatigue, feeling that I have given my best for that day.

☐ I consistently feed my own motivation by spending time with others who are intensely focused on growing and achieving more.

☐ I set aside time at least once every month to reflect on or meditate about my purpose and goals for intensifying my desire.

Principle 11: Discontentment

☐ I have identified the gaps between where I currently am and where I want to be within the next six months (either professionally, socially, spiritually, physically, or financially).

☐ I leverage discontentment in my life as a motivator to make changes for the better.

Principle 12: Pain

☐ I can identify pain or disappointment that is symptomatic of a deeper problem I need to address in order to fulfill my greatest potential.

- [ ] When faced with a major setback or failure, I accept it and look for the hidden opportunity or benefits.
- [ ] When faced with a significant problem, I confront it directly and use its personal impact to intensify my commitment to take action.
- [ ] Instead of avoiding interpersonal conflict, I confront it and seek to become a better person as a result.
- [ ] I do not blame others or circumstances for my problems, realizing instead that every problem contains the seeds of an equivalent or greater benefit.
- [ ] I acknowledge my shortcomings and failures quickly, instead of blaming, defending, or denying.

Principle 13: Enthusiasm

- [ ] Most days, my level of enthusiasm for my life, work, and relationships is above a "7" on a scale of 1–10 (with 10 being the highest).
- [ ] Others would probably describe me as someone who gives them energy because of my enthusiasm.
- [ ] Others would rarely, or never, describe me as a complainer.
- [ ] My enthusiasm comes from positive expectations for the future.
- [ ] I am aware of and manage (or avoid) situations that will steal my enthusiasm for my work, life, and relationships.
- [ ] I use physical, mental, emotional, and/or spiritual disciplines to build and maintain my enthusiasm.

Principle 14: Persistence

☐ I accept setbacks and failures as part of my life journey, and I don't let them destroy or compromise my vision for the future.

☐ I am aware of times when I feel like quitting, and I intentionally decide to keep moving forward toward my vision and goals.

☐ When I feel that I have let myself or others down, I accept it as the past and don't let it prevent me from recommitting to a better future.

☐ When circumstances or people have frustrated and discouraged me, I refuse to play the role of a victim and give away my power for the future.

☐ I revisit my vision and goals at least once a month to renew and sharpen my focus.

☐ Based on a consideration of my experiences, I believe I am more persistent in pursuing my greatest potential today than I was 12 months ago.

Principle 15: Listening

☐ I don't interrupt others or finish their sentences for them.

☐ I don't listen with the primary intent of correcting others or impressing them by how I respond.

☐ In most conversations, I listen more than 50 percent of the time.

☐ I believe I listen well enough to be an advocate for the person who is speaking.

☐ Most of the time, I listen carefully to my spouse or closest friends without wandering mentally or pretending to listen.

☐ When I disagree with another person, I slow down and take time to confirm that I understand them fully before stating my position.

Principle 16: Friendship

☐ I value friendship in and of itself.

☐ I have helped at least three friends with a personal need within the last thirty days.

☐ I have made at least three new friends over the last thirty days.

☐ I have hugged someone other than a family member within the last week.

☐ I don't talk in a friend's absence differently than I do in his presence. In other words, I don't gossip or criticize when he is not present.

☐ I have at least one friend who would give up a weekend to help me deal with a big problem or need in my life.

Principle 17: Energy

☐ I exercise at least five days a week, including both aerobic and weight bearing activities.

☐ I drink at least eight glasses of purified water each day.

☐ I consistently sleep over seven hours each night.

☐ I don't eat more than 20 percent of my calories from packaged foods.

☐ I eat at least five servings of fruits and vegetables every day.

☐ I take one or more antioxidant supplements daily.

☐ I practice deep breathing at least three times per week.

Principle 18: Faith

☐ My spiritual life is an important source of wisdom, guidance, and motivation for me.

☐ My spiritual beliefs have been melded both by holy writings and personal experience.

☐ My spiritual beliefs challenge and appeal to my better self, rather than justify or excuse undisciplined behavior.

☐ I believe I am happier, stronger, and more purposeful as a person because of my spiritual beliefs.

Principle 19: Prayer

☐ I pray and ask for guidance and strength almost every day.

☐ I pray out loud with someone else at least three times per week.

☐ Listening for God's inner voice is an important part of my times of prayer.

☐ I believe I have seen specific, tangible answers to my prayers.

☐ I believe my prayers are answered, even if it isn't always in the way or time that I want.

☐ I consistently pray for others.

Principle 20: Transformation

- ☐ I apologize and ask for forgiveness out loud when I have failed myself, others, or God.
- ☐ I deliberately agree with the truths, principles, and standards of conduct stated in the Scriptures.
- ☐ I have consciously and intentionally forgiven someone else for hurting me in the past 30 days.
- ☐ When I decide to change a behavior or attitude, I follow this decision with a new behavior or attitude.
- ☐ I have shared my shortcomings with another person and asked them to pray with me within the last six months.
- ☐ I view myself as someone loved and forgiven by God, rather than being regularly tormented by a sense of failure and guilt.
- ☐ I am able to forgive myself for my failures and weaknesses.

Principle 21: Relationship

- ☐ I can say that I have experienced and felt God's presence within the last 90 days.
- ☐ My times of worship intensify my awareness of the spiritual realities in my life and circumstances.
- ☐ I have more self-control and peace as a result of my relationship with God.
- ☐ I feel prompted with new guidance as a result of listening for God's voice and direction.
- ☐ I follow through and take action based on the spiritual guidance I receive.

Principle 22: Gratitude

☐ I have told someone "thank you" within the last 24 hours.

☐ I have written at least three "thank you" notes to others within the last 30 days.

☐ In five minutes, I could make a list of 20 reasons why I am thankful.

☐ If someone recorded all of the words I spoke in a day, my expressions of gratitude would outnumber my complaints by at least five to one.

☐ At this moment, I feel blessed and have more of a sense of gratitude than a feeling of frustration, disillusionment, or unhappiness.

Principle 23: Giving

☐ I enjoy giving of my time, talent, or resources to others or a particular cause.

☐ I give at least 10 percent of my income away each month.

☐ I regularly give to those who have less than me, without any thought to their ability to give something in return.

☐ I have given something positive, either tangible or intangible, to someone I don't like or someone who has opposed me within the last 30 days.

☐ I look for opportunities to give or contribute without any expectation of being recognized.

Acknowledgements

There is nothing accomplished in our lives without help. I am grateful to these folks who have both inspired and assisted me in this project:

Sharon Brooks, for her many years of friendship, assistance, and trustworthiness,

Maryanna Young and the Aloha Publishing team, for their expertise, enthusiasm, and belief in our message,

Kelly Antonczak, for her creative ideas and working with the details of the manuscript,

Justin Foster, for his strategic clarity and refreshing wit,

Stacy Ennis, for her editing skills,

Nick Zelinger, for the interior design of the book,

Cari Campbell, for the amazing cover design,

Sherri Linsenbach, for her very professional indexing skills,

The many authors, speakers, coaches, and friends that have nourished me throughout the years,

My wife, Pam, who is full of the Treasure Inside,

And most of all, to God, who has not given me what I deserve but, instead, has given me so much that I don't deserve.

Join the Treasure Inside Community

Deepen your understanding of each of the 23 Principles by joining the Treasure Inside Community.

Visit **www.treasureinsidebook.com** for resources that will help you put the book's principles into practice in your life.

+ Action Steps for implementing the 23 Principles

+ Stay connected with us on LinkedIn at **www.linkedin.com/in/treasureinside**

+ "Like" the Treasure Inside Facebook Page here: **www.facebook.com/treasureinsidebook**

To learn more about Ron Price and other products and services, visit **www.price-associates.com**

Discovering Your Natural Talents

Benefit from over 30 years of Ron Price's research on understanding and developing natural talent!

Tools that capture and deliver Ron's research findings:

- **Personalized Video Coaching**
  - On-line behavioral style assessment that provides information on the general characteristics of your behavior, the value you bring to the organization, and keys to communicating, managing and motivating.
  - Immediate access to personal assessment results.
  - 23 video responses to help you understand your personal report.
  - Report and video coaching can be reviewed at any time.

- **TriMetrix™ HD Talent Profile**
  - Online assessment that provides comprehensive insights into your naturally recurring patterns of thought, motivation and behavior for ongoing learning and development.
  - Includes self-assessment of your mastery of 25 different leadership skills, plus insights on how to increase your leadership capabilities.
  - A detailed personalized report.
  - Live coaching is also available.

- **Emotional Intelligence Report**
  - Online self-assessment that measures your emotional intelligence for a better understanding of your Emotional Quotient (EQ).
  - A detailed personalized report that will help you leverage your awareness of emotions for effectiveness in the workplace.

To learn more about Ron Price
and other products and services,
visit **www.price-associates.com**

Recommended Reading

Oatmeal v Bacon: How to Differentiate in a Generic World
By Justin Foster
Aloha Publishing, 2011

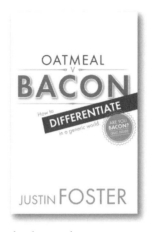

Oatmeal is boring. Bacon is interesting. This metaphor brings clarity to why some brands dominant and others survive. *Oatmeal v Bacon: How to Differentiate in a Generic World* makes the case that earning attention and market share starts by being a truly unique and interesting brand. Humorous, thought provoking and full of useful ideas, *Oatmeal v Bacon* will transform the way you market and advertise, develop products, create customer experiences, and build a culture. Most of all, *Oatmeal v Bacon* will give you permission to be yourself and build a brand around being truly different.

Conversations for Change: 12 Ways to Say It Right When It Matters Most
By Shawn Kent Hayashi
McGraw-Hill, 2010

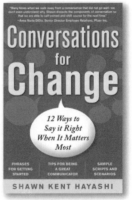

Whether you're trying to motivate a team, negotiate a contract, make a sale, ask for a raise, land a new job, or terminate an employee, the conversations you have will either help you succeed or undermine your goals. Communication expert and leadership coach Shawn Kent Hayashi has spent more than two decades studying how the things people say impact their business and professional lives. In her new book, *Conversations for Change: 12 Ways to Say It Right When It Matters Most*, she not only identifies the twelve most important types of conversations people have, but shows readers how to reach their maximum potential by using these conversations effectively.

The Page – Ten Powerful Ideas to Transform Any Business
By Randy Lisk
The Clark Group, 2008

Randy Lisk's playbook to organizational improvement is unique because its strategies also work on a personal level, encouraging individuals to examine their personal and management effectiveness. With an engineer's sense of clarity and logic combined with more than seventeen years of consulting, Randy has designed a no-nonsense foundation for building and sustaining an effective organization. This book does not promise "five steps to overnight success;" instead, it challenges the reader to think deeply and encourages people to create a future that can sustain challenges and inevitable change.

Leadership Simple, Leading People to Lead Themselves
By Steve and Jill Morris
Imporex International, 2003

Get great results from everyone you lead. Turn everyone into a leader. Imagine leading an organization where every person thinks and acts like a leader, where each individual takes ownership for what they and their team produce, and accountability is the glue that keeps people focused on what really matters. If you want to create this vision in your team or your organization, this book provides the tools to make it real.

The books on this recommended reading list are available on Amazon in both print and e-reader versions.

Find more information on Ron's recommended reading list at **www.price-associates.com/store**

About the Author

Ron Price is an internationally recognized business advisor, speaker, and author. Known for his creative and systematic thinking, business versatility, and practical optimism, Ron has worked in 15 countries and served in almost every level of executive management over the past 35 years. As the former CEO of a multi-million dollar international company, Ron understands the challenges and risks of running a business and building a dynamic team. He works shoulder-to-shoulder with executive leadership teams in small, family-owned businesses to Fortune 100 global companies, helping bring strategic clarity and transformational results—especially those dealing with turmoil and transition. In 2004, Ron started Price Associates, a leadership development firm that features the bright minds and innovative solutions of some of the world's top consultants in organizational development, process management, branding/marketing, and more.

Ron is part of the International Faculty of Target Training International, Ltd.™ (TTI) and a TTI Chairman's Club member. Ron and Price Associates were the 2006 recipient of the TTI TriMetrix® User of the Year Award and the President's Award for Superior Performance. In 2008, Ron was honored with the TTI Coach of the Year Award and, in 2009, was presented with awards for Services to the Community and for Superior Performance. In 2011, Ron received the TTI Bill Brooks Impact Award for his commitment and contributions to the industry and the TTI network. Ron is also a Certified Professional Behavior and Values Analyst and a Consultant in Good Standing with the Hartman Institute at the University of Tennessee. He is certified as a Business and Christian Values Profile Axiologist from The Value Source Group. Ron is also a member of the Odyssey Global Leadership team, a group of 100 consultants worldwide who have been trained in delivering transformational programs for businesses. Ron has been using the Odyssey Transformational Strategies with organizations in the U.S. and China since 2006.

A member of the National Speakers Association, Ron has traveled more than one million miles, giving more than 1,000 speeches in 15 countries. His ability to connect with an audience is one of his strongest assets.

With a blend of creative thinking, limitless energy, and business expertise, Ron helps enhance individual and organizational effectiveness, profitability, and growth through a combination of the following:

1. **Business Advisor** – to have the conversations you can't have with anyone else.
2. **Facilitator** – to create conversations that trigger a mindset change.
3. **Executive Tool Kit** – to provide effective tools for organizational performance.
4. **Expert Outsourcing** – to connect clients with great leaders.
5. **Speaker** – to engage audiences with relevant content and inspiration through keynotes, workshops, and leadership development programs.

To connect with Ron, visit www.price-associates.com or www.treasureinsidebook.com.

Index

Notes

Notes

Notes

Notes